Inquire, Investigate, Integrate!

Making Connections to the K–2 Science Standards and the Common Core

T0308146

By Kaye Hagler

Inquire, Investigate, Integrate!
Making Connections to the K-2 Science Standards and Common Core
by Kaye Hagler

© 2014 Kaye Hagler
All rights reserved.

Cover Illustration: Cynthia Akiyoshi
Composition/design: Studio Montage

Photo Credits
Shutterstock: Johan Larson, cover, throughout (leaf), Matthew Cole, cover, throughout (magnet), Nataliya Hora, cover, throughout (cell background), romrf, cover, throughout (magnifying glass)

Library of Congress Cataloging-in-Publication Data
>
Hagler, Kaye R.
Inquire, investigate, integrate! : Making connections to the K-2 science standards and common core
by Kaye Hagler
pages cm.
ISBN 978-1-62521-516-1 (pb)
1. Science—Study and teaching (Elementary)—Standards—United States. I. Title.
LB1585.3.H34 2014
372.35'044—dc23 2013037146

Maupin House publishes professional development resources for K-12 educators.
Contact us for tailored, in-school training or to schedule an author for a workshop or conference.
Visit www.maupinhouse.com for free lesson plan downloads.

Maupin House Publishing, Inc. by Capstone Professional

1710 Roe Crest Drive
North Mankato, MN 56003
www.maupinhouse.com
800-524-0634
352-373-5546 (fax)
info.maupinhouse.com

Printed in the United States of America in Eau Claire, Wisconsin.
102013 007819

For all children who look at life and ask "Why not?"
or "What will happen if I. . .?"
And to all teachers who give their students the time,
patience, and tools to seek their own answers.

To Clara, Tammy, Anika, Rhonda, Lara and the first graders
at Lynn Haven Elementary for their assistance
and to Terry for his untiring support.

Introduction

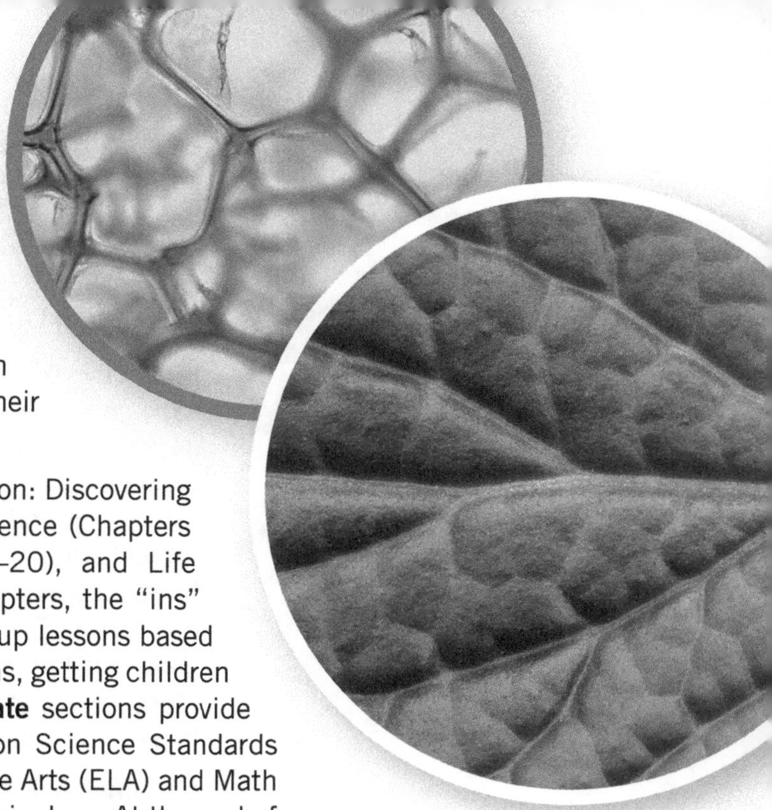

Inquire, Investigate, Integrate! begins with the "big idea" that Earth is a unique place in the universe, one with diverse landforms and life-sustaining properties. From there, students are taken on a journey that ultimately leads them to consider their own unique qualities and place in this world.

Chapters are grouped into four key units of instruction: Discovering the World of Science (Chapters 1–4), Physical Science (Chapters 5–11), Earth and Space Science (Chapters 12–20), and Life Science (Chapters 21–25). Within each of the chapters, the "ins" (Inquire, Investigate, and Integrate) are used to group lessons based on their content. **Inquire** sections act as introductions, getting children to consider the chapter inquiry question. **Investigate** sections provide science activities with a focus on NEXT Generation Science Standards (NGSS). **Integrate** sections provide English Language Arts (ELA) and Math activities, supporting children's skills across the curriculum. At the end of each unit, two assessments are provided: one for beginning students and one for advanced students. Assessments include a combination of multiple choice (for standardized test practice), short answer, and inquiry-based, open-ended prompts.

Breaking It Down

Inquire: Introductory Activities

Each chapter begins with at least one Introductory Activity. These activities are designed to pull students into the chapter content and activate their curiosity and imagination. They usually address some of the NGSS and often address ELA or Math Common Core State Standards (CCSS) as well. In order to determine which standards are addressed, consult Appendix B.

Investigate: Science Activities

The science activities in this book address NGSS, released in April of 2013. According to the National Science Teacher Association, the standards "establish learning expectations for students that integrate three important dimensions—science and engineering practices, disciplinary core ideas, and crosscutting concepts." (Appendix A discusses the development and thinking behind NGSS.)

Integrate: ELA and Math Activities

Few things stand in isolation, and content areas are no exception. The Integrate activities in this book (while they involve scientific thinking and often work with the science activities) address ELA and Math CCSS. For example, the ELA CCSS emphasize explanatory text-based writing, a skill necessary for the needs of a process-/inquiry-based science curriculum.

Likewise, measurement in a science classroom or laboratory would not be possible without mathematical principles. Appendix B provides correlations between each lesson in this book and the Science, Math, and ELA standards.

Additional Instructional Features

Interactive Dialogue and Discussion Points. The Inquire lessons that launch each chapter include "Interactive Dialogue," scripts that teachers can use as they introduce and explore the Inquiry Question; these scripts are provided only as an instructional aid, and their use is optional. After the instruction portion of the introductory lessons (and in many other lessons throughout the book), "Discussion Points" are provided to extend and clarify the concepts under investigation. They are provided as *starting points* for discussion. Each classroom is different, and no one ever knows what may come out of the mouths of babes. Questioning is where true learning begins. (Just ask Aristotle!) So if Taylor, Alex, Haley, or Amy go off-topic with their line of questioning, rein them out, but don't cut them loose.

Multimedia Inspiration. Each chapter includes at least one list—titled "Inspire"—that suggests additional media that could be brought into the lesson, such as video clips and units of study (retrievable online), relevant nonfiction/informational texts, and thematically related fiction texts. You are encouraged to have students use the Internet when online research opportunities appear in the text. When possible, consider allowing students to produce their work using a word processing program or drawing program instead of pencil and paper.

Responses to Input from Teachers. The content of Appendix D—lesson-related activity sheets—was created and refined in response to feedback received from classroom teachers who were kind enough to test-drive this work. As a first-grade teacher was looking over a first draft, she requested that I pull the charts and graphs from the chapters and place them in the back for ease of use, whether as copies or projectables. So I did that. Another elementary teacher's request that I place all word-wall terms together in a separate appendix resulted in Appendix C, which contains chapter-by-chapter vocabulary. A third teacher asked that I boldface vocabulary/word wall terms within the text to indicate they are explained. So I did that as well. Last but not least, a teacher requested that I supply both a higher-level and a lower-level assessment for each unit, so I did that. As you can see, the design and format of this work was driven by the needs of those who know best: classroom teachers. I am grateful for their input, and I believe that you will be as well.

Appendices. To aid in instruction, four appendices (each mentioned briefly above) are provided at the back of the book:

- **Appendix A** contains research that supports the structure and thinking behind the development of *Inquire, Investigate, Integrate*, along with a list of suggested further readings.

- **Appendix B** contains an easy-to-follow guide to correlations between the text and the standards. All critical-thinking, inquiry, and hands-on activities included in the 25 chapters correlate with NGSS. All ELA and Math activities (along with several introductory and science activities) correlate with CCSS for ELA and Math. All standards are grouped by unit, chapter, and activity title.
- **Appendix C** contains a vocabulary/word wall list, including all science terms by chapter.
- **Appendix D** contains graphic organizers, posters, and other useful activity sheets that can be copied and distributed to students or presented using, for example, an interactive whiteboard.

Science Notebook. Throughout this book, students are encouraged to record results, describe objects, formulate questions, or create foldable learning aids. Many of the instructional aids in Appendix D can be inserted into the notebook.

One Final Point

Lessons throughout the text should always be adapted to the needs of the learner. Feel free to modify them as you see fit. Most important, feel free to enjoy the experiences that are coming your way!

Table of Contents

Unit Two: Physical Science

Unit 1

Discovering the World of Science

Chapter 1

What in the World?

Chapter Inquiry Question: What makes our world a special place?

Chapter Vocabulary/Word Wall: landforms, observe, world

Inquire: Introductory Activities

Introductory Activity 1.1: Our World

Difficulty Level: Beginner

Objective: Examine the surface and shape of Earth

Supplies: Globe, large map of Earth, pictures of different landforms, and (optionally) access to Google Earth

Interactive Dialogue

Listen carefully to the following expressions:

- *What in the world?*
- *Yum, that dessert was out of this world!*
- *When she received the award she was on top of the world.*

What do all those sayings have in common? (The word *world*.) *We use the word* ***world*** *when we talk about everything on our planet as one thing.*

Our world has mountains and seas, tropical rain forests, deserts, canyons and grasslands. These are called ***landforms****. Landforms are natural features and shapes found on the Earth's surface. Our world also has plants, animals, and people. It has you. We all are part of this world, Earth. Our world is called Planet Earth, and there is no other world like ours.*

- *What do we call this world?* (Earth)
- *Does anybody know what shape our world is?* (round)
- *Can you name other objects that are round?* (Responses will vary.)

Let's look at, or ***observe****, our world more closely as we think about Earth's many kinds of landforms.*

Instruction

Show pictures (e.g., from the Internet, magazines, textbooks, or pictorial atlas) of various landforms found on Earth, such as mountains, deserts, grasslands, canyons, and plains. Use the following discussion points to help engage your students.

Discussion Points

- Landforms and bodies of water found on Earth
- The shape of the world/Earth
- Places students might like to visit: an iceberg, an island, a canyon, or a waterfall
- Natural events that might have shaped Earth

Extension: Encourage students to find photos (personal, magazines, online) that show a landform. For example, photographs taken while on vacation might include landforms in the background (ocean, Niagara Falls, Black Hills). Arrange photographs on a bulletin board under a landform heading.

Difficulty Level: Beginner

Objective: Provide an interactive, imaginative journey around the Earth

Supplies: Imagination!

Introductory Activity 1.2: Hot Air Balloon Ride

Interactive Dialogue

Let's take a hot air balloon ride! Imagine what it would be like to ride in a hot air balloon and travel all over the world. Think of all the things you would see!

Let's pretend that we are going to take a journey around the world in a hot-air balloon. Imagine that you are floating along around the world, keeping your eyes and ears open to everything around you. Are you ready? Hold on to your seats!

The first thing we need to do is wave goodbye to everybody below us. Ready? Goodbye! Goodbye!

Oops! We need to float a little higher because we are about to cross over a tall __________. (mountain)

Burr! It's cold up here. It feels like it is going to __________. (snow)

Now let's float a little lower. Look to your right. There's a whale swimming in the __________. (ocean)

Now look to your left. Look! There's a herd of elephants. Duck! They are about to spray us with water from their __________. (trunks)

It's getting really hot here. I see monkeys and long twisting vines. I think we must be near a __________. (jungle)

It's time for us to head back home. Raise your hand if you see something else you would like to share with the class. (Responses will vary.)

Instruction

As desired, add even more motions—such as shooing the birds when they get too close or coughing as you pass a volcano. Continue to encourage children to add their own observations from their seats on the balloon.

Inspire★

As time allows, follow this activity with a video of an actual hot air balloon (many are available online) or with a class read-aloud, such as *Hot Air Balloon* by Mari Schuh or *To Fly in the Sky* by Layne deMarin.

Investigate: Science Activities

Science Activity 1.1: Colors of the World

Difficulty Level: Beginner

Objective: Visually portray the surface area of Earth; it comprises more water than land

Supplies: Small coffee filters, green and blue washable markers, squirt bottle(s) of water, paper plates, globe/representations of Earth, black construction paper, copies of the activity sheet "My World" (Appendix D, page 168)

Instruction

Begin this investigation with a discussion of Earth's surface. Tell your students that Earth's surface has much more water than land. In fact, water covers almost 70% of Earth's surface! To help students visualize the ratio of water to land, they will create a color representation of the top layer of the Earth's surface.

Step 1: Each student (or group) places one small coffee filter onto a paper plate.

Step 2: Looking at a globe, photograph, or map of Earth, they color the filter in blue and green, trying to create a pattern of water to land that is similar to the model's.

Step 3: Students squirt a small amount of water—only one squirt—in the center of the filter.

Step 4: Students wait for about 10 seconds and then observe what happens!

Step 5: After the filters have dried, students can glue or tape them to the activity sheet "My World" and add the page to their Science Notebook.

Step 6: Beneath the filter have students write the following: "The surface of the Earth is 70% water."

Difficulty Level:
Beginner
(with Advanced Extension)

Objective: Demonstrate that the Earth's surface contains more water than land

Supplies: Inflatable Earth globe (or a beach ball colored 70% blue and 30% green to represent the Earth's surface), 2-column chart (large enough to share with the class) labeled "Land" and "Water" for recording the results of the experiment

Science Activity 1.2: Earth Toss

Instruction

This activity can be conducted in the classroom with students remaining in their seats or outside with students in a large circle.

Explain to students that today's activity will help them experience just how much more water than land covers the earth. Remind them that 70% of the Earth's surface is water, explain the activity, as below, and then begin:

Step 1: The class will toss the globe (or beach ball) back and forth.

Step 2: When students catch the ball, their hands should remain in the place where they landed.

Step 3: After each catch, a checkmark will be added to the chart—under "Land" if the student's right thumb is on land (a green or brown area) and under "Water" if the thumb is on water (a blue area). Continue the investigation in this manner until the ball has been tossed to all students.

Step 4: Tally the results. How many marks are under "Water"? How many marks are under "Land"?

Extension: Use the results of the activity to determine the class's percentage of water to land. How closely do the results reflect that 70% of the Earth's surface is covered with water? (If so, the ratio of checkmarks under "Land" to those under "Water" will be 3:7.)

Difficulty Level:
Advanced

Objective: Determine the location of various landforms (e.g., deserts) around the world and use symbols from a map key to show where the landforms appear

Supplies: Copies of the activity sheet "Match the Landform" (Appendix D, page 169)

Science Activity 1.3: Landforms

Instruction

Model the activity, working through the first item as a whole group.

Explain to students that the numbers on the map match the numbers in the list, and show where each feature appears on the earth. For example, a glacier exists on the surface of the earth where the #1 is marked on the map. After determining where the glacier belongs, students can use the key at the bottom of the activity sheet to find the symbol for glacier. Then, they can draw that symbol in the correct location on the map. Have individual students or small groups continue the exercise. After the activity, discuss the results with students using the questions below.

Discussion Points

- Why would one place have a desert and another place have a rain forest?
- Why isn't there a glacier close to where we live?

Integrate: ELA and Math Activities

ELA Activity 1.1: A New Kid in Town

Difficulty Level:
Beginner

Objective: Imagine and draw a student from Glorf

Supplies: Paper and crayons/colored pencils

Interactive Dialogue

Imagine! A new kid has just walked into the classroom. He doesn't look like someone from our world because he is from Glorf, a strange, faraway place. Let's describe him together and draw our new classmate.

1. *His head is shaped like a _________.*
2. *He doesn't have ears; he has _________.*
3. *Instead of eyes like we have, he has _________.*
4. *He doesn't have any hair on his head; he has _________.*
5. *His body is shaped like a _________.*
6. *Instead of two arms, he has _________.*
7. *His clothes are quite different from what we would wear because he _________.*
8. *He doesn't walk; he _________.*
9. *Would you be his friend? Why?*

Instruction

Provide paper and drawing supplies. Have students draw a line down the middle of the paper. On one side they will draw their alien from Planet Glorf, using the descriptions the class developed. If you like, students can draw as you describe the student together. On the other side, students will draw a person from Planet Earth. As students' skills allow, encourage them to label each side of their drawings, "Earthling" and "Glorf-ling." Have students keep their drawings to support the ELA activities that follow.

Inspire★

- The storybook *The New Kid from Planet Glorf* by Arie Kaplan supports this lesson.
- *The Ocean Story* by John Seven explores the clash between natural and man-made objects in Earth's oceans.

ELA Activity 1.2: Letter from Earth

Difficulty Level:
Advanced

Objective: Write a letter using descriptive language

Supplies: Pencils and paper

Instruction

Explain to students that they are going to pretend they are the new student from Glorf. How would they feel as a new student in this strange land called Planet Earth? While they pretend to be the new student, they are going to write a letter to their friends back home on Planet Glorf. In this letter they are to describe this strange, new world. Remind them that as an alien they do not know words like *mountain* or *river*. They need to describe this world with brand new eyes, using descriptions for things instead of labels/names.

Difficulty Level: Advanced

Objective: Write and illustrate a comparison/contrast paragraph

Supplies: Paper and pencils, colored pencils or crayons

ELA Activity 1.3: Glorf Compared with Earth

Instruction

Distribute drawing supplies and let students know they will be drawing the Planet Glorf. After they have finished drawing Planet Glorf, they will make a chart showing similarities and differences between the two planets. Finally, they will write a paragraph to compare Planet Glorf with Planet Earth.

As students begin drawing, help get their ideas flowing: *What does Glorf look like? What shape is Planet Glorf? Is it round like Earth? Earth's colors are blue, green, and brown. What are the colors of Glorf? What are Glorf's special landforms?*

Once they have a drawing of Glorf, they can make a chart or Venn diagram showing the similarities and the differences between the two planets. Travel around the room, supporting students' efforts to identify similarities and differences.

Finally, students can write their paragraphs, explaining how the two worlds are different and how they are the same.

Modification: This activity can be performed as a modeling activity for the comparison/contrast paragraph format, using students' ideas as you create a Venn diagram and write the paragraph.

Difficulty Level: Advanced

Objective: Write a persuasive letter

Supplies: Paper and pencils, colored pencils or crayons

ELA Activity 1.4: Save Planet Earth!

Instruction

For this activity, students will write another letter to people back on Planet Glorf. This time, students are to imagine that they are an alien from Glorf who really likes this new world, Earth, and who has made many new friends here.

Have students write a letter to the people who live on Planet Glorf explaining that Earth is a friendly planet and not an enemy. Glorf should not invade Earth as it once planned to do. In their paragraphs, students should give three reasons why Glorf should not invade Earth.

Modification: Use this activity as a modeling opportunity for persuasive writing, paying particular attention to transitions, such as *also* and *in addition*.

Difficulty Level: Advanced

Objective: Use measuring devices

Supplies: Tape measures, a collection of spherical objects

Math Activity 1.1: Measure Up!

Instruction

Students will work in teams with measuring tape to measure the distance around the largest part of a spherical object (soccer ball, Ping-Pong ball, baseball). Each team will make a chart listing each object and the number of inches/centimeters measured. They will enjoy measuring other interesting objects—like their heads! Depending on students' skill levels, the word *circumference* could be used in the conversation.

Chapter 2

It's Only Natural!

Chapter Inquiry Question: How are natural objects different from man-made objects?

Chapter Vocabulary/Word Wall: man-made, natural

Inquire: Introductory Activity

Introductory Activity 2.1: Natural vs. Man-Made

Interactive Dialogue

Our Planet Earth is an amazing planet! On our balloon journey, we saw many kinds of landforms: oceans, glaciers, mountains, and deserts. These are all part of nature. If it is part of nature, it is a ***natural*** *object. Machines did not make sea shells or pine cones because they are part of __________.* (nature)

You won't find a screwdriver growing from a tree. You won't see a television swimming in the ocean. The screwdriver and the television are ***man-made*** *objects, and we don't find them in nature. But if we think about it, we realize that it takes natural objects to make man-made objects! Natural objects can be changed into man-made objects.*

Let's observe this spoon. It is made of wood that came from a tree, but it has been cut and sanded to make a wooden spoon. It has been changed from a natural object to a man-made object.

A clay pot is another example. Clay comes from the earth, usually from areas where rivers or streams once flowed. Clay pots are one of the earliest man-made objects. People started making them a long, long time ago because they needed a way to carry water. They discovered that if they shaped clay and baked it in a fire, then they would have a nice, solid pot. The clay was changed from a natural object to a man-made object.

Who can think of another man-made object? (Responses will vary.) *Can you think of the natural objects that were used to make this man-made object?* (Hold up each item from the collection.)

Difficulty Level: Beginner

Objective: Demonstrate the difference between a natural object and a man-made object

Supplies: Wooden spoon, clay pot, assortment of natural and man-made objects or pictures, copies of the activity sheet "Natural/Man-Made" (Appendix D, page 170)

Extension: Early American colonists who lived near the seashore crushed seashells and limestone, among other materials, to make tabby, a material used to build their homes. Invite a builder to school to discuss with students various building materials that are used today.

Instruction

Distribute copies of the activity sheet "Natural/Man-Made." To model the activity, create a 2-column chart where all students can see it; label the columns "Natural" and "Man-Made." From their seats, have students look around and "spy" a natural object. Then, write the name of the object (or if possible, allow a volunteer to do so) under the heading "Natural." Next, have students "spy" a man-made object and write (or, again, have a volunteer write) the object's name under the chart heading "Man-Made." Encourage students to copy these items onto their activity sheets and add more items that occur to them. They could be added to their Science Notebooks.

Extension: Provide photographs that include both natural and man-made objects and work as a whole group to "spy" objects belonging to each category.

Discussion Points

- What do all natural objects have in common?
- What do all man-made objects have in common?
- What natural objects might have been used to create some of the man-made objects listed on the chart?

Inspire★

- Consider screening the video *The Potters of San Marcos: The Clay and the Pot*, which is available on the History for Kids website. This video shows the process of using clay to make a pot.
- You might also want to have on hand a book to use for a whole-group read-aloud, such as *Natural and Man-made* by Angela Royston.
- Literary/fiction texts thematically related to this chapter's content include the following texts:
    - *The Blue Stone Plot* by Susan Blackaby
    - *The Forest Surprise* by Carla Mooney

Investigate: Science Activities

Science Activity 2.1: Sponge Power

Interactive Dialogue

Sponges found in the ocean are living animals. They attach themselves to an object; then, they hold on and grow! Deep-sea divers gather, or harvest, sponges in the same way that people pick vegetables in a field.

People buy sponges for various uses. What are some ways that we can use sponges? (Cleaning, painting, etc.) *Some people use them like a paintbrush or to apply makeup.*

Instruction

Distribute copies of the activity sheet "Science Experiment: Natural vs. Man-Made Sponge," giving one copy to each student or team. Following the experiment, students can glue or tape the chart into their notebooks. (Note that this activity can be combined with Math Activity 2.1: Sponge Experiment Data.)

Organize students into teams with one sponge of each type and guide them to perform the following tests:

1. Softness Test: Run the sponge across the back of the hand, across the face, and along the arm. Discuss the results as a team and place a check mark showing which sponge feels softer.
2. Smell Test: Take a deep whiff! Which smells the best? Discuss and record the results.
3. Soak Test (Absorbency):
   - Measure 1 ounce (or 30 ml) of water.
   - Pour water onto the surface of a table or on the floor and lay a man-made sponge on top of the water. Lightly press the sponge against the water. Squeeze the water into the cup or beaker and measure the water.
   - Be sure the surface area is completely dry. Then, conduct the same experiment with the natural sponge.
   - Discuss and record the results: Which sponge soaked up, or absorbed, more water?

Discussion Points

- Why was one sponge more absorbent (or able to soak up more water) compared with the other?
- Teamwork is important in a group activity. What did you do that helped you conduct your experiments as a team?

Difficulty Level: Beginner

Objective: Conduct an experiment comparing an ocean sponge (a natural object) to a manufactured sponge (a man-made object) that has been designed to be similar to the natural object.

Supplies: Natural sponges and synthetic sponges of approximately the same size, measuring cup or beaker, bottle of water, copies of the activity sheet "Science Experiment: Natural vs. Man-Made Sponges" (Appendix D, page 171)

Difficulty Level:
Beginner

Objective: Collect objects and determine whether each belongs in the "Natural" category or in the "Man-Made" category

Supplies: Small paper lunch bags, small plastic sandwich bags (to be used as gloves), paper plates, two buckets (one labeled "Natural" and one labeled "Man-Made"), 2-column Natural/Man-Made chart large enough to share with the class, clean copies of the activity sheet "Natural/ Man Made" used in a previous activity (Appendix D, page 170)

Science Activity 2.2: Nature Walk

Interactive Dialogue

What is natural and what is man-made? Today we are going to walk slowly around the playground and search for small objects that are either man-made or natural.

You might find a tiny pebble, a small stick, a piece of paper, a plastic bottle cap, a leaf, or a blade of grass. Use your plastic bag like a glove to collect the objects you find. Place them into your paper bag.

We don't collect living organisms like bugs or worms. We don't collect anything sharp like glass, and we don't collect animal poop. We also don't pick leaves or petals from plants for this science investigation. Let's collect only those that have fallen to the ground. That way we won't be hurting any plants.

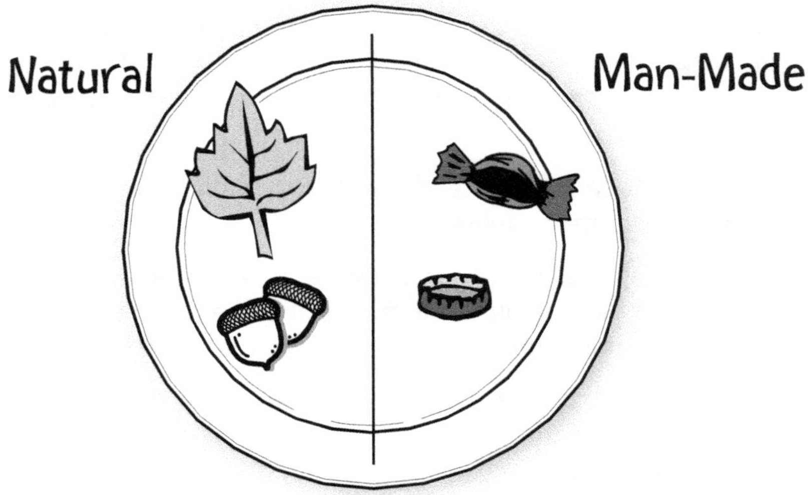

Instruction

Make arrangements for a nature walk either on the school playground or at a local park. Before leaving the classroom, have students write their name on one side of the paper bag in bold colors. Review the terms *natural* and *man-made*. Show an example of each.

After the nature walk, distribute paper plates and instruct students to draw a line down the middle, labeling one side "Natural" and the other "Man-Made." Students will then sort their collection into two groups according to the labels.

After sorting their objects, individual students will bring their plates one at a time to the front of the classroom and share their findings. As students place each of their items in the correct bucket, list each item on the large 2-column chart (Natural/Man-Made) that resembles students' activity sheets. Each time an object is mentioned again, place a check mark beside the object's name on the chart.

Distribute copies of the activity sheet "Natural/Man-Made." In each column, students will list (or draw) the four items from the class chart that have the most check marks.

Discussion Point

- If many man-made objects were found on the walk, how can each person can help to keep the world free of litter?

Natural	Man-Made
leaf ✔✔✔	pencil ✔
pine needle ✔	candy wrapper ✔✔
rock ✔✔	bottle top ✔

Integrate: ELA and Math Activities

ELA Activity 2.1: The Potter

Difficulty Level: Advanced

Objective: Determine the main idea and sequence of events in a nonfiction text

Supplies: The book *Clay* by Mary Firestone, pencil and paper, newspaper or plastic place mats cut from disposable tablecloths

Instruction

Before reading aloud the book *Clay*, let students know that the listening goal is to discover the steps necessary for creating a pot from clay. Tell them that after the reading, the class will work together to list the steps on the board in the order in which they are performed.

Once the list of steps has been created, students will protect their tables or desks with newspaper or plastic mats. Then they will use the clay as they follow the posted steps for creating a small pinched pot or coiled pot. (If you are using a SmartBoard, print instructions for table partners.)

Math Activity 2.1: Sponge Experiment Data

Difficulty Level: Advanced

Objective: Use real calculations to create a number sentence using the mathematical symbols *greater than* and *less than* (> and <)

Supplies: Chart paper, whiteboard, or pencils and paper

Instruction

This activity is an extension of Science Activity 2.1: Sponge Power and/or Science Activity 2.2: Nature Walk.

Discussion Points

- In the sponge experiment, was the number of teams that liked the natural sponge "greater than" or "less than" the number of teams who did not like the sponge?
- Was the number of man-made objects found greater than or less than the number of natural objects found?
- Rewrite the results on the board using the < and > symbols (e.g., the number of teams who liked the natural sponge > the number of teams who liked the man-made sponge).
- Reverse the direction of the number sentence (e.g., the number of teams who liked the man-made sponge < the number of teams who liked the natural sponge).
- Continue the comparisons with other class findings (e.g., the number of leaves found > the number of bottle caps found).

Chapter 3

Natural Processes

Chapter Inquiry Question: Why is change necessary in the natural world?

Chapter Vocabulary/Word Wall: experiment, natural process, sprout

Inquire: Introductory Activity

Difficulty Level:
Beginner

Objective: Demonstrate the use of questioning as a strategy through the exploration of a natural process

Supplies: Photographs showing natural processes (e.g., snow falling, waves crashing, birds flying)

Introductory Activity 3.1: Natural Processes

Interactive Dialogue

When water falls to the ground from the sky, we might say, "Hey, it's raining outside!" Rain is an example of a natural process, something that happens without anyone's help. No machine is used, and it isn't man-made. We don't make rain fall. We also do not make ocean waves move. These are examples of ***natural processes****, or things that happen without help from people. Even a bird eating a worm is a natural process. It must eat to grow and have energy, and people do not have to make it eat or give it food. Who can name another natural process?* (Responses will vary.)

Think of the sun.

- *What does the sun appear to do every evening?* (go down/set)
- *What does the sun do every morning?* (rises)
- *What does a caterpillar change into?* (butterfly)
- *What does a bear do in the winter?* (sleeps/hibernates)

Each of these events that occur in nature—eating, growing, sleeping, moving, changing— is part of a __________ __________ (natural process).

Instruction

Show photographs of natural processes. Instruct students to look at each photo carefully for one minute and to think of different questions about the picture. For example, for a picture of a seashell in the sand, they might ask questions, such as:

- How did the seashell get in the sand?
- Did something live in the shell?

Model this questioning technique for children before turning them loose to create their own questions. You may wish to set the ground rule that each student should contribute only two questions. This will prevent the activity from being monopolized by a few students. It will also encourage children to think carefully and share their very best questions.

Extension: Have students bring in pictures of a natural process that are visible to them in a one-day period. Then, they can create questions based on their photos. For example, questions springing from a photo of a sunrise might be: How do the colors change across the sky? Why are the colors red, orange, and yellow?

Inspire

- Search the Internet for time-lapse photography showing a natural process, such as a flower blooming, seasons changing, or a plant growing. The National Geographic website offers several such videos: moving clouds, changing tides, and melting glaciers. Emphasize for students that these clips show natural processes.
- Rudyard Kipling created several storybooks that will support the discussion of myths later in this chapter:
    - *How the Rhinoceros Got His Skin*
    - *How the Leopard Got Its Spots*
    - *How the Elephant Got Its Trunk*
    - *How the Camel Got Its Hump*

Investigate: Science Activity

Difficulty Level: Beginner

Objective: Observe a natural process (seeds sprouting)

Supplies: Variety of seeds (e.g., sunflower, pinto, corn, bean), small plastic bags, paper towels, construction paper, markers, rulers, stapler, spray bottle of water, eye dropper, copies of the activity sheet "Natural Process: Seeds Sprouting" (Appendix D, page 172)

Science Experiment 3.1: Sprouting Seeds

Interactive Dialogue

Today we are going to learn about one natural process—seeds sprouting. We are going to answer the question "If we plant four different kinds of seeds, will they all ***sprout****, or start to grow, at the same time?" We are going to conduct an experiment to find out!*

An ***experiment*** *is a test that we can use to explore an idea or answer a question. After we answer our question about whether seeds take the same amount of time to sprout, you will get to find answers for your own question. What do you want to discover about the seeds in our experiment?* (Responses will vary.)

Instruction

This activity is designed as a small-group (team) activity, but you can adjust it to work for the whole group, for pairs, or for individuals.

Distribute one small plastic bag and a seed to each team. Instruct students to write the name of their team and the name of their type of seed (e.g., bean, sunflower) along the top of the bag with the marker. Next, they will add a small amount of water to the bag and close it tightly. Let the seeds soak overnight.

The next day, each team will remove its seed from the bag and pour out the water. One member of the team will get one sheet of paper towel and dampen it slightly using the spray bottle of water. The seed and paper towel will then be placed into the bag and sealed with the seed visible from the outside.

Teams will design and build their greenhouses, using construction paper or other materials. The greenhouses should be wider and taller than the plastic bag. They can cut a triangle to fit on top for the roof. Each team should label its greenhouse with "Our Greenhouse" (or "My Greenhouse"). They can decorate the greenhouses with markers or attach seed packets or pictures.

Each day, students will place a few drops of water on the paper towels to keep them slightly moist. They will record data for this experiment on the activity sheet "Natural Process: Seeds Sprouting" and add the activity sheet to their Science Notebook.

Extension: Create a chart showing the types of seeds used and the number of each that sprouted. Which type of seed sprouted first in this test?

Discussion Points

- What did students notice about the size of the seeds over time?
- Why did some seeds sprout and others not sprout?
- If the seed was left in the bag, would it continue to grow into a healthy plant? Why or why not?

Extension: After sprouting the seeds (or as a replacement activity), students can plant their seeds in containers full of dirt, find a sunny location for them, and monitor their growth.

Extension: A visit to a local greenhouse could serve as a follow-up to this activity. Emphasize that greenhouses provide an environment that supports growing plants.

Integrate: ELA and Math Activities

ELA Activity 3.1: Creating Myths

Difficulty Level: Advanced

Objective: Explore myths, sequencing, and narrative writing

Supplies: Paper, colored pencils, storybook

Interactive Dialogue

How do natural processes begin? For example, how did birds first know how to fly? Why did birds begin eating worms? Long ago, people would create stories to explain natural processes. We call those stories myths. Here is a story, or myth, about fire. It is called "Father Sun."

Read the following myth aloud, reminding students to notice the order of the events in the story.

Father Sun

Once, Father Sun saw a bear walking on Earth. The Sun was very hungry, and the bear looked good to eat. Father Sun pulled off a long ray of light and threw it at the bear. Oops! He missed.

Father Sun's ray landed in a grassy field. The field caught on fire. Another oops!

Quickly, Father Sun called on his friend Rain to put out the fire. But it wasn't long before Sun threw another ray and threw it down to Earth! And that is how we got fire!

Is this how we really got fire? (No.) *Myths are not real-life stories, so whenever we know that something is a myth, we know that not all of information is true.*

Instruction

After the story, have students look at the pages of a typical storybook. (The myths listed in the Inspire section earlier in this chapter would all make excellent choices.) Point out that the story follows a sequence of events: It shows what happened first in the story and then what happens next and next until finally the end is reached.

Myth Foldable

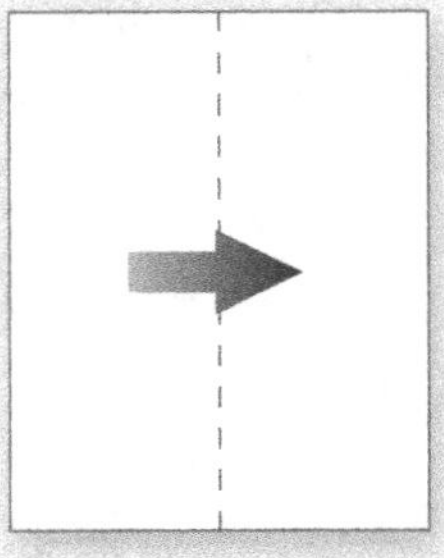

Step 1: Fold a sheet of paper in half lengthwise (hot dog).

Step 2: Fold the paper a second time (hamburger)

It should look like this at the completion of step 2.

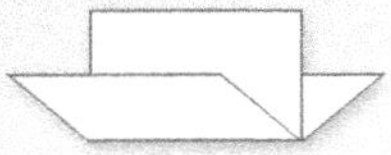

Step 3: Fold each section up to the fold line (think bird).

Turn on its side and reopen.

For this activity, students will use the "Myth Foldable" process, as shown in the drawing, to create a mini-book. Once the book is complete, the students will design the front cover and number the pages of their books. The drawings on the four interior pages of the book will be as follows:

1. A picture of Father Sun throwing a ray of light toward a bear.
2. An unhappy Sun seeing fire on the ground.
3. Rain pouring down on the fire.
4. Father Sun getting ready to toss another ray.

Instruction

After students have created a picture book for the myth, they can create their own story about a different natural process (e.g., the blooming of a flower, a rainbow, waves moving across the ocean).

Students will first plan, or draft, their stories on another sheet of paper before writing or drawing their final story. They will follow the same steps as in the "Myth Foldable" activity above. Remember, creativity rules!

Math Activity 3.1: Fractured Math

Interactive Dialogue

Let's say we planted 20 seeds and only 10 sprouted. We could say that 10 out of 20 seeds sprouted.

What if on a fishing trip your family catches 5 fish? You caught 2 of them, or 2 out of 5.

5

Here's another example: While walking along the beach, Aisha and Bethany collected 12 seashells. Aisha found 7 of the 12 seashells.

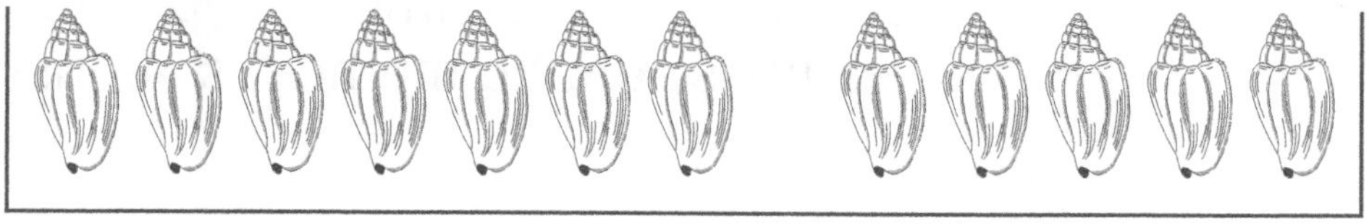

12

We have a special way of writing numbers, such as our 10 out of 20 seeds that sprouted. This special way of writing numbers is called fractions. The word part ***frac*** *means "break." If you break an arm or leg, we say that you* ***frac****tured your bone.*

We can also break numbers, which is what we do when we say that ten out of 20 of the seeds sprouted. Let's use our fish example. The total number of fish was 5, but that number was broken or ***frac****tured when we said that you caught 2 of them. We can show broken numbers by creating a fraction. Fractions show one number over, or on top of, another. So when you caught 2 out of the 5 fish, we can write the broken number like this:* $\frac{2}{5}$ *For the seashells, Aisha caught 7 out of 12 of them, and we write that number like this:* $\frac{7}{12}$.

Now let's return to our sprouts example. We said that 10 out of 20 seeds sprouted. How would we write the broken number? ($\frac{10}{20}$) *When we write broken numbers in this way, we create a fraction. A fraction shows a number broken into two parts.*

Instruction

Write the numbers from the interactive dialogue as fractions on the board. Next, have each student write one "fractured math" problem. (For example, "We have 3 pets. Two of them are cats.") They can pass their problem to a partner to express as a fraction.

As time allows, have students continue creating additional fraction word problems working with different objects, such as food items or comic heroes.

Difficulty Level:
Advanced

Objective: Explore fractions and word problems

Supplies: Pencils and paper

Chapter 4

Be a Scientist!

Chapter Inquiry Question: How do scientists conduct an experiment?

Chapter Vocabulary/Word Wall: conclusion, experiment, hypothesis, results scientific method, scientist

Inquire: Introductory Activity

Difficulty Level: Beginner

Objective: Discover the role of a scientist

Supplies: Pencils and paper, scissors, copy of "Scientific Method" poster (Appendix D, page 173), copies of the activity sheet "Scientific Method" (Appendix D, page 174)

Introductory Activity 4.1: The Role of a Scientist

Interactive Dialogue

(You may wish to display the "Scientific Method" poster as you move through the Interactive Dialogue.)

Remember when we made up made-up stories, or myths, about natural events? Of course, none of those events really happened. Father Sun did not toss its ray to earth to kill a bear. That's not how we got fire. There are people, however, who know the real answers to questions like "How did we get fire?"

*A **scientist** is a person who knows about and tries to learn more about natural processes. Scientists ask questions about the natural world around them. Then they experiment to find the answers to such questions as why the sun comes up each morning, what plants need to grow, and why our breath stinks, and why milk builds strong bones! When they investigate, scientists use the **scientific method**, which includes six very important steps:*

1. *They observe a problem or something they don't understand about nature, people, animals, and natural processes.*
2. *Next, they ask a question. Why does a seed sprout, a flower bloom or rain fall? Why do we sneeze or burp? What keeps a flying bird from falling out of the sky?*

3. *Next, they form a hypothesis. Suppose a scientist said: "A seed sprouts because it gets sun." This is a* ***hypothesis****, or a possible answer to the question.*
4. *The scientist would then test that hypothesis. In other words, she would conduct an* ***experiment****, or investigation. "Wait a minute!" the scientist might say. "The seed received plenty of sunshine, but it still didn't sprout."*
5. *The* ***results*** *of this experiment are what happened. The next step for the scientist is to study the results. The results for the sprout experiment showed that more than just sunshine was needed for a seed to spout. Now the scientist might start all over again looking for the right answer to the question.*
6. *After more testing, the scientist gets to the last step in the scientific method. He or she develops a final, or last, answer. We call this final answer to the original question a* ***conclusion****. The last step in the Scientific Method is to state a conclusion.*

Instruction

Distribute the "Scientific Method" activity sheet to students. Support students as they write the steps in the scientific method. When the work is done, students can add the activity sheet to their Science Notebooks.

Discussion Points

- If students could be scientists for a day, what would they like to investigate?
- What are some questions scientists might ask?
- How does questioning help to solve real-world problems?

Extension: Here's an easy way to discover what it's like to be a scientist in space. Put on a pair of large gloves and try to perform simple tasks like placing the top on a bottle. This will illustrate some of the challenges faced by scientists in space (astronauts).

Inspire★

- Students can "Go Mad" as they enjoy a read-aloud with *Mad Margaret Experiments with the Scientific Method* by Eric Braun, or they can explore the world of scientists through easy-to-read biographies.
- A mingling of information and photographs of famous scientists all come together in a unique video "Scientific Method Rap" available online.
- The literary/fiction text *Science Fair Nightmare* by Sean O'Reilly offers a unique perspective on the experiences of a young "scientist."

Investigate: Science Activity

Difficulty Level: Beginner

Objective: Design a water filter system

Supplies: Bucket of muddy water; empty water bottles cut in half; paper cups; funnels or paper to roll into funnels; rocks (big enough that they won't fit through the bottle tops); tiny pebbles/gravel; material for students' filters (e.g., sand, cotton balls, paper towels, coffee filters); copies of the activity sheet "Cleaning Up Dirt and the Scientific Method" (Appendix D, page 175)

Science Activity 4.1: Cleaning Up Dirt

Interactive Dialogue

The water that comes from our faucets has been cleaned to make it safe to drink. It comes from underground wells and from lakes and rivers.

Our water is cleaned by a system of machines that filter, or take out, the dirt, rocks, and other things we don't want to drink.

Before people use machines for important processes like cleaning our water, the machines have to be tested. Scientists build a ***model****, or a small copy, of the real machine to test how well it works. Then they test the machine. Let's make our own model of a water filtration system and see how well it cleans some muddy water!*

Instruction

This investigation can be conducted as a whole class, by teams, or by partners. Before beginning, distribute the activity sheet "Cleaning Up Dirt and the Scientific Method." Work through the beginning of the activity sheet with students, using the following questions:

- What do students observe in the bucket? (muddy water)
- We cannot drink dirty water, so what is the big problem? (The water is muddy.)
- What question needs to be asked? (How can we clean up the water?)
- How can this problem be solved? (Students provide their hypotheses and write them on the activity sheet under "How can I solve this problem?")

Now students are ready to perform the experiment:

Step 1: Students select two items—sand, cotton balls, paper towels, or coffee filters—that they think will make the best filter. Then, they will record their choices on the activity sheet.

Step 2: Next, students will insert the top half of the bottle upside down into the bottom half.

Step 3: In the top half of the bottle, students layer first rocks and then gravel, then their selected two materials.

Step 4: Once they have built their model filters, students will use the paper cup and funnel to pour muddy water over their filter.

Step 5: Next, they will observe the results and record them on their activity sheets.

Step 6: If microscopes and magnifying glasses are available, students can examine small drops of water even more closely.

Step 7: Remove the filters (i.e., the top halves of the bottles) and set them aside. Line up the bottles of water and provide time for students to compare the results of all filters.

Discussion Points

- Which two materials made the best filters?
- What problems did you experience while conducting the experiment?
- If you were to conduct the experiment again, what changes would you make?

Integrate: ELA and Math Activities

ELA Activity 4.1: What's the Big Idea?

Difficulty Level: Advanced

Objective: Develop a "big idea" in informational writing

Supplies: Books or videos about the life of one particular scientist, such as *Everyone is a Scientist* by Lisa Trumbauer, one copy of activity sheet "KWL Chart" (Appendix D, page 176)

Interactive Dialogue

Today we are going to write about scientists. Let's make a list of facts we already know about scientists. We will write these facts in our "Know" column. (Student responses will vary.)

For our next column, let's brainstorm about other things we "Want" to know about scientists. (Again, student responses will vary.)

Finally, in this last column we will write facts we "Learn" about scientists. As we go through our book (or video), listen for information that we can place in this column.

Instruction

After all columns have been completed, continue to work together as a class to develop one "big" or main idea about scientists based on the information in all three columns. If your students are not ready to write independently, this activity can serve as a modeling opportunity as you work with students to craft the "big idea" sentence and the details that support it.

Math Activity 4.1: Pizza Party!

Difficulty Level: Advanced

Objective: Use deductive reasoning to compare a scientific process to a mathematical process

Supplies: Brain power, pencils and paper

Instruction

Provide an opportunity for students to practice deductive reasoning with the following question: How is solving a problem in math like solving a problem in science?

Explain that scientists and mathematicians (or people who do math) both go through steps to arrive at a conclusion. Various math problems can be used to illustrate that the steps in the scientific method are used in solving a math problem.

Problem: Three friends are coming over for a pizza party. You know that everyone will want to eat two slices of pizza. There will be four people at the party, counting you. The pizza that you ordered is already cut into eight slices.

Question: How many pizzas do you need to order?

Form a hypothesis: The party will surely need two pizzas.

Conduct the experiment: Place two slices of pizza beside each person's name.

Study the results: 8 slices

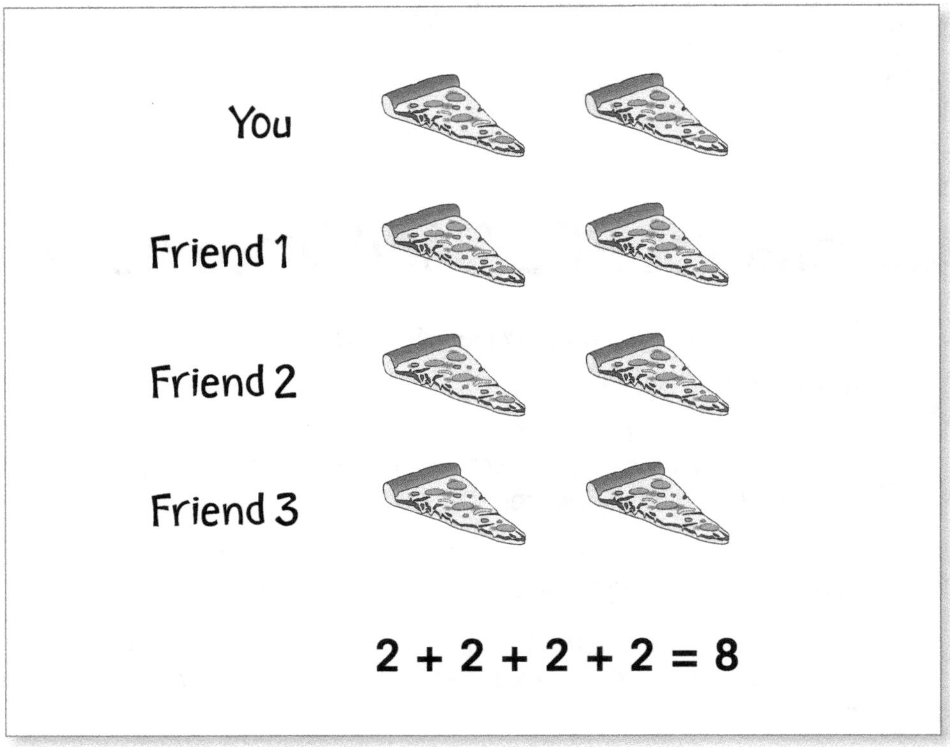

Develop a conclusion: One pizza is all that will be needed!

Extension: How many pizzas would you need to order if five people were coming to your house? Eight people? Work through the new problems, again using the vocabulary of the scientific method.

Name: ______________________________

Unit 1 Assessment (b)

1. Color Earth's land and water.

2. Name or draw a natural object.

Name or draw a man-made object.

©2014 Kaye Hagler from *Inquire, Investigate, Integrate*. This page may be reproduced for classroom use only.

3. Circle the letter that does not show a landform.

a. 

b. 

c. 

d. 

4. Circle the letter that shows a drawing of a natural process.

a. 

b. 

c. 

d. 

5. What does a scientist do? Write a list or draw a series of pictures that show the many things a scientist will do to solve a problem.

©2014 Kaye Hagler from *Inquire, Investigate, Integrate*. This page may be reproduced for classroom use only.

Name: ____________________

Unit 1 Assessment (a)

Select the letter that best answers each question.

1. What covers most of Earth's surface?
   a. water
   b. land
   c. mountains
   d. deserts
2. Which of the following is a man-made object?
   a. bowl made of clay
   b. vine
   c. seashell
   d. bird nest
3. Which letter does NOT contain only landforms?
   a. rivers, seas, valleys
   b. mountains, cities, lakes
   c. oceans, deserts, hills
   d. pond, canyon, cliff
4. Which of these activities is a natural process?
   a. a kite that is flying around
   b. an egg that has been scrambled
   c. a bird building a nest
   d. a drawing of a family
5. Which choice shows words a scientist would NOT USE in describing the scientific method?
   a. color the landform
   b. make an observation
   c. form a hypothesis
   d. conduct an experiment

Dig-Deeper Questions:

6. Why are landforms in one area different from landforms found in other places in the world? ____________________
7. How can a puddle of mud be both a natural and a man-made object?
   ____

©2014 Kaye Hagler from *Inquire, Investigate, Integrate*. This page may be reproduced for classroom use only.

8. Select any natural process. Draw this process in action.

9. Is a soft drink better than water for growing a plant? ______________

a. What would be your hypothesis? ______________________________

____

b. Describe or draw the steps in an experiment you might use to answer this question. (You may use the chart in your Science Notebook to help with this answer.)

Open-ended Inquiry Question:

10. What makes Earth a special place?

 ©2014 Kaye Hagler from *Inquire, Investigate, Integrate*. This page may be reproduced for classroom use only.

Unit 2

Physical Science

Chapter 5

What's the Matter?

Chapter Inquiry Question: What are the properties of the three states of matter?

Chapter Vocabulary/Word Wall: gas, liquid, matter, property, solid, state

Inquire: Introductory Activity

Difficulty Level: Beginner

Objective: Demonstrate the three states of matter

Supplies: Assortment of different colored blocks, a feather, bottle of water, cup, clear round vase or pot, a small inflatable flotation device (like those attached to children's arms while they swim), a copy of the poster "Three States of Matter" (Appendix D, page 177)

Introductory Activity 5.1: Solids, Liquids, and Gases

Interactive Dialogue

Follow my instructions. Take hold of your hair and pull gently! Now pull your right ear. This time pull your left ear. Next, hold out your right arm, then your left arm. This time I want you to reach out as far as you can and grab a handful of air. Hey! There's nothing in your hand! Where's the air?

Hum, there's something the matter here. In fact, science is all about "matter." ***Matter*** *is anything that takes up space. We can say that taking up space is an important* ***property*** *of matter, or a way to describe it. So what's the matter? I am matter! I take up space. You are matter! You take up space. This block is matter! It takes up space. This cup is an example of matter in a solid* ***state****, or way of being. Matter can exist in any of three states: solid, liquid, or gas.*

(Show students the poster "Three States of Matter" while presenting information on the properties of the three states of matter.)

- *A* ***solid*** *is matter than can keep its shape like these blocks. A solid doesn't change unless we melt it or burn it. It can be a rock or a chair! A solid can be heavy like a brick. (Pantomime picking up a brick.) Or it can be light as a feather! (Pick up the feather and blow it into the air.)*
- *A* ***liquid*** *is different. An important property of liquid, like this water, is that it takes the shape of its container, the bottle. Now watch what*

happens when I pour this water into a container with a different shape. The liquid changes its shape as well. A liquid can be the shape of a cup or a bucket or a crooked river or a small pond or a tall waterfall. (Make the motion of a waterfall.) It can be wide as the ocean. (Hold your arms straight out to the sides.) It can be round like a small pot. (Bring your hands together to form a cup.)

- *A* ***gas*** *can also take the shape of its container. One way gases are different from liquids is that many gases cannot be seen. Hold the palm of your hand in front of your mouth. Now blow! Do you feel your breath? It is a type of gas. You can't see your breath unless it is really cold outside. Watch what happens when I blow into this float. See the shape it makes? The gas inside—my breath—takes the shape of its container. This time, it goes in a circle so that we can slip it over our arms and go for a swim.*

Discussion Points

- What are examples of solids found at home? Liquids? Gases?
- Name a liquid that can be changed into a solid. (cake batter into cake layers, cream into butter, flavored gelatin from liquid to solid)
- What caused these changes to occur? (adding heat, taking away heat)
- Name a solid that can be changed into a liquid. (ice cube, ice cream) What caused the change? (heat)
- Name a liquid that can be turned into a gas. (a puddle of water in the sun, boiling water) What caused the change? (heat)

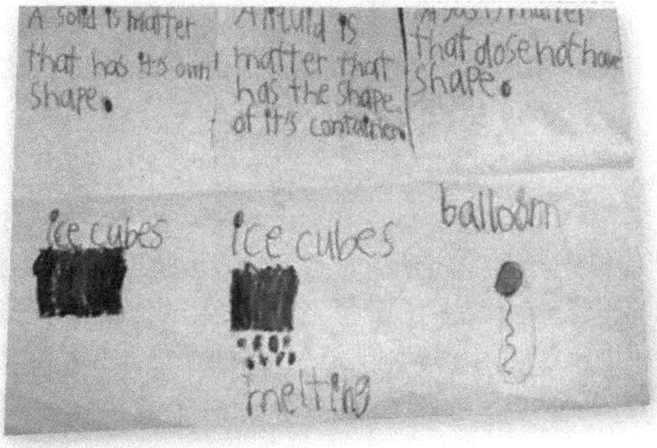

Extension: Students can create a Solid, Liquid, Gas foldable and place in their Science Notebooks.

Inspire★

Visualize the concept of the changing states of matter with one (or more) of these resources:

- *Joe-Joe the Wizard Brews Up Solids, Liquids and Gases* by Eric Braun
- The video "Solid, Liquid, Gas," available on the Science Kids website

Investigate: Science Activities

Difficulty Level: Beginner

Objective: Observe the changing states of matter

Supplies: Ice cubes made from an assortment of fruit-flavored drink mixes and natural juices, plastic sandwich bags, strong tape

Science Activity 5.1: A Cool State of Matter

Instruction

Have students closely observe the ice cubes and review the properties of the solid state of matter. Distribute plastic bags to students and have them write their name along the side. Give each student the same number of fruity ice cubes. They will place the cubes in the bag and then find a nice sunny window (or other warm spot) to set them in. The bags should be securely taped to the surface.

Periodically, have students check the bags and watch as the cubes gradually melt and change into a liquid state. As students continue to monitor their experiment, they may begin to notice water droplets forming near the top of the bags. If it was allowed to escape, it would turn into the third state, a gas.

Discussion Points

- What would happen if you opened the bag slightly?
- Why did some ice cubes melt more quickly than others?

Difficulty Level: Beginner

Objective: Visualize the property that gas takes up space

Supplies: Straw, plastic sandwich bag, duct tape, lightweight books

Science Activity 5.2: Air Power

Instruction

Gas as a state of matter is not always as easily understood as solids and liquids. This activity offers another way to visually demonstrate gas's property of taking up space.

Have students insert a straw into a sandwich bag. Move it to the side of the bag. Close the bag tightly all the way to the straw. Put a small piece of tape by the straw to seal the bag tightly around it. Next, have students place a light book on top of the sandwich bag. They will then lean down and blow into the straw. Watch out for falling books!

Discussion Points

- What happened to the book?
- What caused the book to move? (air or gas)

Investigate: Science Activities

Science Activity 5.3: Bubble Science

Instruction

If you intend to make your own bubble solution, a number of videos can be found online providing directions. "Bubble Power" on the Science Discovery website is an excellent example. This is the solution: 10 parts water to 4 parts liquid dish detergent and 1 part white corn syrup. Avoid overmixing the liquids.

Assist students as they make bubbles by dipping their wands into the bubble solution and waving the wands around. Students will enjoy observing the various shapes the bubbles take—at least until they break free—based on the solid objects (i.e., the wands) used. For closer observation, distribute hand-held magnifying glasses.

Discussion Points

- What solids worked best for making bubbles? Why?
- How does size affect the strength of a bubble?
- What does a bubble look like through a magnifying glass?

Difficulty Level: Beginner

Objective: Combine liquid objects (the bubble solution) and solid objects (the bubble wands) to create an assortment of "containers" (bubbles) for a gas to fill (air)

Supplies: Buckets; water; shallow pans; liquid bubble solution; objects to use as bubble wands (e.g., slotted spoons, six-pack rings, rings from jar lids, fryer baskets, coat hangers twisted into shapes)

Investigate: Science Activities

Science Activity 5.4: Raising Raisins

Interactive Dialogue

In this experiment, we will identify a solid, a liquid, and a gas.

First, look at the cup in front of you. What state of matter is the cup—solid, liquid, or gas? (solid) *Next, let's pour the soft drink into our cup. What is the state of matter that we are pouring?* (liquid)

Now, we each need to count out five raisins. What state of matter is a raisin? (solid)

When I say go, gradually drop the raisins into the liquid. Ready, set, go! Now, watch carefully. What is beginning to happen? (Bubbles) *Continue watching. Now what is happening?* (The raisins are floating to the top.)

The soft drink contains a gas called carbon dioxide. We can't see it, but it's there. The gas is being pulled out of the soft drink and attaching itself to each raisin. It carries the raisin to the top of the soft drink.

Discussion Points

- Would using water instead of soft drink give the same results? Why?
- Would a different solid instead of the raisins provide the same results? What if marbles were used?

Difficulty Level: Advanced

Objective: Observe the process of a gas rising

Supplies: Clear drinking cups (4-ounce size or larger); fresh, clear soft drink; raisins

Extension: Have students develop and test a hypothesis that uses a different solid. As a whole class, discuss *why* certain solid objects worked and others did not.

Integrate: ELA and Math Activities

Difficulty Level:
Beginner

Objective: Create a step-by-step list of instructions for a science experiment

Supplies: Pencils and paper

ELA Activity 5.1: Science Reporter

Instruction

Students will write or draw a list of the steps they used to conduct one of the experiments in this chapter. They should write a title at the top of the page. Next, students will write a main sentence that explains the purpose of the experiment. Then, they should record the steps, numbering them in the order in which they were performed. The Science Notebook can be used for this activity.

Extension: Using their growing knowledge of transitions (e.g., *next, after, before, first, then*), students can underline them in their steps.

Difficulty Level:
Beginner to Advanced

Objective: Use measurement tools

Supplies: Assortment of objects to be weighed and measured (e.g., books, blocks, stones), glue sticks, small rulers, beam balance, copies of the activity sheet "Solids" (available in a beginner version and an advanced version; Appendix D, pages 178 and 179)

Math Activity 5.1: Measuring Solids

Instruction

Set up learning stations as described below and provide adult assistance at each station as necessary. Provide each student with one easily weighed object.

Station One: Color (labeled for students to copy)

Station Two: Shape (labeled for students to copy)

Station Three: Measurement

Station Four: Mass/Weight

A variation of this task is to have an assortment of objects available at the Measurement and Weight/Mass Stations. In that case, students can draw an object that is as tall as their own object or draw an object with a similar weight.

Following the activity, students should add their "Solids" sheet to their Science Notebooks.

Extension: What can students learn about their pets? (Pets are solids!) For example, one of the pieces of data taken when a sea turtle is hospitalized is the measurement of its carapace, or shell.

Chapter 6

Mixtures and Solutions

Chapter Inquiry Question: How does a mixture differ from a solution?

Chapter Vocabulary/Word Wall: mixture, solution

Inquire: Introductory Activity

Introductory Activity 6.1: All Mixed Up!

Difficulty Level: Beginner

Objective: Demonstrate properties of a mixture and a solid

Supplies: Mixer, small box, assortment of small items (e.g., screws, washers, paper clips, rubber bands), sugar, water, large-mouth jar with cheesecloth secured across the top with a rubber band

Interactive Dialogue

Does anyone know what this tool is? (mixer) *What is the purpose for a mixer?* (mix things together). *At home, you might use this to make pancakes or cupcakes. When we combine different or similar types of matter, we often have a mixture. A* ***mixture*** *is a combination of things that do not change when they are combined; in other words, a mixture can be broken back down into its parts, and the parts are not changed.*

Let's mix together some of the solids I have gathered and place them into this box. We can now say we have a ***mixture*** *because if we separate the items, taking them out of this box, each item is still the same. They did not change.*

When we put different or similar states of matter together and mix them so well that you can't see the separate items any longer and you can't easily take them apart again, we have a ***solution****. Examine these two states of matter: Our liquid is water, and our solid is sugar. What do you think will happen when I mix them together?* (The sugar will disappear.)

Let's experiment and see. Look, the sugar is disappearing. That is because it is dissolving, or changing. The sugar is equally spread out through the water after its been stirred. Even if I strain the solution through this cloth, I can't separate the sugar from the water. When things are combined so that they cannot be easily taken apart again, we have a solution.

Discussion Points

- Where do you think the sugar went?
- Can you think of other examples of mixtures? Solutions?
- How can we tell whether something is a mixture or a solution?

Inspire★

- Read aloud the book *Mixing and Separating* by Chris Oxlade.
- Ready for a little more action? Go outside for some Mixture/Solution fun with the "M and S Rap." Explain that poems—even "raps"—can have the sound of music. Share with students that words to a song are called lyrics. In this activity they will follow the words/lyrics while acting like a mixture and a solution. A teacher or leader can recite the lyrics during the activity until students are familiar with the words. Then they can all join in.

(Begin with everyone twirling and moving around individually)

I'm a mixture!
States of matter
Come together
But nothing's changed
'Cause I'm a mixture!
Bump and rumble
Tumble, toss
We're together but still the same.
Why?
'Cause I'm a mixture!
I'm a mixture!

(Everyone now comes together, joining hands, and move around in a circle.)

Now we come together
'Cause we're making a
Solution!
We're all the same,
All are one.
It's a magical
Solution!

(Everyone slowly falls to the ground without releasing hands.)

That is all;
We've now dissolved,
'Cause we've become
(Whisper) a solution!

Investigate: Science Activities

Science Activity 6.1: Exploration Stations

Instruction

Pairs of young scientists will conduct experiments to discover the difference between mixtures and solutions. The goal is exploratory learning with the freedom to use available measurement tools and varying ingredients. Assign each team a work area to keep students from crowding together.

Students will combine water with other ingredients and then determine whether the result is a mixture or a solution. (If the water and the other ingredient can be easily separated, they have a mixture; if not, they have a solution.) They will use their "Mixtures and Solutions" chart to record their results, but caution them to keep their charts in a dry place and walk back and forth to their charts as they work through the experiment.

Difficulty Level: Advanced

Objective: Conduct experiments to explore mixtures and solutions

Supplies: Squares of plastic tablecloths to protect each station; old shirts/aprons to protect children's clothes; assortment of small containers (e.g., plastic drinking cups, large bowls); pitchers of water; substances to stir into the water (e.g., sugar, sand, oil, cornstarch, rice, powdered drink mixes, salt); items for creating filters (squares of cheesecloth, coffee filters, rubber bands); coffee stirrers or spoons; funnels (or paper to roll into funnels), copies of the activity sheet "Mixtures and Solutions" (Appendix D, page 180)

Integrate: ELA and Math Activities

ELA Activity 6.1: We've Got the Beat!

Instruction

Play a selection of songs for the class. At the conclusion of each, discuss and list on the board the main ideas of the song's lyrics. Next, share thematically linked poems and list their main ideas. Many students will enjoy independently or collaboratively writing a poem about an object in the natural world. As a poem starter, they can begin with the words, "Once there was a ________"

If resources are available, add music and record student performances.

Difficulty Level: Advanced

Objective: Understand how songs and poems are alike

Supplies: Selections of poems and songs that share a theme (like spiders!)

Math Activity 6.1: Measuring Solutions and Mixtures

Instruction

Give one copy of the activity sheet "Measuring Mixtures and Solutions" to each student. Students "fill" the measuring container on the activity sheet ⅓ full using the blue marker. Next, they use their red marker to "fill" the container from ⅓ to ⅔. Last, they use the green marker to color from ⅔ to 3/3. Explain that they now have a full cup. The separate colors show a mixture.

Now it's time to mix things up! Instruct the students to hold all three markers in one hand and simulate stirring by coloring the entire container with all three markers. It's not a mess—it's a solution!

Difficulty Level: Beginner

Objective: Visualize the difference between a mixture and a solution

Supplies: Markers, copies of the activity sheet "Measuring Mixtures and Solutions" (Appendix D, page 181)

Chapter 7

Mass and Falling Objects

Chapter Inquiry Question: Will objects of different weight reach the ground at the same time when dropped?

Chapter Vocabulary/Word Wall: acceleration, mass, weight

Inquire: Introductory Activity

Difficulty Level: Beginner

Objective: Demonstrate Galileo's theory of falling objects

Supplies: Tightly wadded ball of paper, rock, piece of wood molding (preferably with a groove down the center to guide rolling objects)

Introductory Activity 7.1: Free Fall!

Interactive Dialogue

A long time ago, a man named Aristotle had an idea. He thought a heavy object would fall to the ground faster than a lighter object. For instance, a rock would fall faster than this ball of paper.

Many years later, however, another man came along who had a different idea. His name was Galileo Galilei. Like the good scientist he was, he first observed different items dropping to the ground. Second, he asked a question. Do heavy objects really fall faster than lighter objects? Now think back to the scientific method. What is the third thing Galileo did? (Test his idea.) *Let's do the same thing.*

Let's see a show of hands. How many think that this rock will hit the ground faster than this ball of paper? Let's conduct our own test. We will first weigh each object to determine its ***weight****, or how strongly it is being pulled toward Earth by gravity; heavy objects have more weight.* (See chapter 8 for more on gravity.)

Remember when we said we were all made of matter? The ***mass*** *of an object is the amount of matter it has. Sometimes here on Earth weight and matter seem like the same thing because heavy objects (or objects with more weight) often have more mass as well. I am heavier and have more mass than you. An elephant is heavier and has more mass than I do.*

Let's consider our ball of paper and this rock. Which weighs more? (The rock.) *That's right, the rock has more mass.*

Instruction

Create a chart on the board to record the weight of each item. Next, drop both items at the same time. Following this first experiment, use other paired items (e.g., a shoe and a book, a sock and a pencil). Be sure to always weigh items first and record the weight on the chart.

Discussion Points

- Why do objects with different weight hit the floor at the same time?
- Is there a more scientific way to prove this?

Inspire★

- Revisit the world of Galileo at "Galileo's experiment at Leaning Tower of Pisa" available from NASA/Langley Research Center.
- Learn more about measurement with the book *How Do You Measure Weight?* by Thomas K. Adamson and Heather Adamson.
- Explore the book, *Science Measurements: How Heavy? How Long? How Hot?* by Chris Eboch.

Investigate: Science Activities

Science Activity 7.1: On Your Mark, Get Set, Go!

Difficulty Level: Beginner

Objective: Determine the speed of a moving object

Supplies: Ramp made from a board (preferably with a groove down the middle) or cardboard (lightly creased down the middle), or some other material, such as a cardboard cylinder; stack of books to create an angle/prop at the high end of the ramp; ruler or piece of wood to stop the objects at the bottom of the ramp; assorted balls of different weights (e.g., Ping-Pong balls, tennis balls, golf balls); stopwatch; copies of the activity sheet "Falling Objects" (Appendix D, page 182)

Interactive Dialogue

Once our scientist Galileo knew he was right about objects of different weights falling at the same time, he realized he had another problem. Objects fell so quickly he couldn't tell how fast they were going. Bam! The whole experiment would be over. So he asked more questions: How can I measure the speed of falling objects? How can I slow the speed down so it can be measured? If you were Galileo, what would you have done? (Responses will vary.)

When drivers want their cars to go fast, what do they do? (Press down on the gas pedal.) *Pressing down on the gas pedal, or accelerator, lets them go faster.* ***Acceleration*** *is an increase in speed. When they want to slow down, what do they do? (Step on the brake.) A car's brakes will slow down its speed.*

Here's what Galileo decided to do. He conducted an experiment using a ramp to slow down the speed of moving objects. That's what we are about to do.

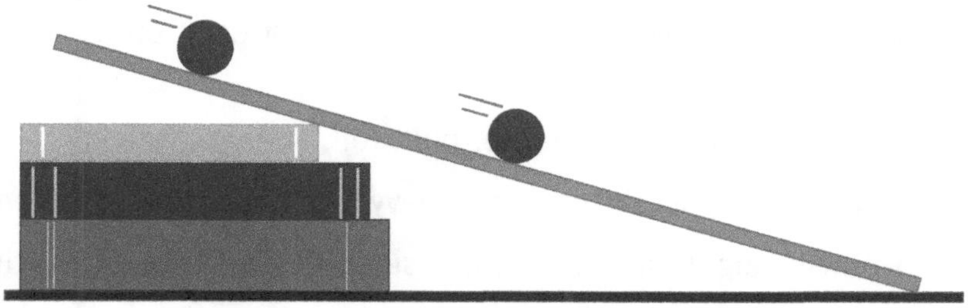

Instruction

Line up pairs of objects. Have students predict which object will get to the bottom in the least amount of time. Before each test, weigh the objects. Then, use the "Falling Objects" activity sheet to record the timed runs with a stopwatch.

Continue the experiment by raising the upper end of the ramp to increase acceleration. Again, poll students as to their observations: will speed increase if the ramp is raised even though the distance is the same? Why? Following the activity, students will add their sheets to their Science Notebooks.

Discussion Points

- Which objects seemed to be slower?
- Did an object's weight, or mass, affect the time it took to roll down the ramp? Why?
- Why did raising the ramp's upper end increase the speed?
- What would have happened if nothing had been placed at the bottom of the ramp?

Difficulty Level:
Advanced

Objective: Vary the angle of a slope to change the speed of an object

Supplies: Cardboard tubes (paper towel or toilet paper rolls), duct tape, cups, cardboard, marbles, scissors, glue, stopwatch

Science Activity 7.2: The Marble Challenge

Instruction

Form teams. The students in each team will work together toward one objective: Build a structure that will keep a marble rolling for the longest time possible. Think roller coaster! Record the timed runs on a class chart.

Discussion Points

- What problems were encountered in the experiment?
- How were these problems solved?

Integrate: ELA and Math Activities

Difficulty Level:
Advanced

Objective: Use verbs, adjectives, and nouns to write sentences related to the chapter's theme

Supplies: Scissors, tape, pencils and paper, copies of the activity sheet "Sentence Cube Template" (Appendix D, page 183)

ELA Activity 7.1: Sentence Cubes

Instruction

Students will work in teams to create three different word cubes. Each team will need to cut out three "Sentence Cube Templates" (or two for an easier challenge). Using words from this chapter, students will list adjectives in one cube, verbs in the second cube, and nouns in the third cube. Teams will need to select six words for each cube. Some examples are provided below.

Verbs: fall, drop, accelerate, pull, roll, change, weigh

Adjectives: fast, slow, equal, heavy, light, unequal, different

Nouns: weight, size, mass, measurement, speed, object, time

The words will be written in the squares of the cube. Next, students will fold and tightly crease along the dotted lines. Finally, they will pull the sides up and tape along the edges. The top will then be pulled down and taped. Voila! A perfect cube!

The fun begins when all three cubes are rolled. Provide a certain amount of time for students to create and write as many sentences as they can with the three words. They may work separately for a little competition or cooperatively.

- Students may add more words to make a complete sentence.
- Students may use the word in any form. (e.g., rolled, pulls)
  Example: roll, slow, mass
  The mass of the big ball made it roll slowly.

Math Activity 7.1: Recording the Results of an Experiment

> **Difficulty Level:** Advanced
>
> **Objective:** Find the difference in timed trials
>
> **Supplies:** Completed student copies of the activity sheet "Falling Objects" (Appendix D, page 182)

Instruction

In Science Investigation 7.1: On Your Mark, Get Set, Go! students used stopwatches to time the objects as they rolled down the ramp. Using the results from that experiment, find the differences between the two times. This same activity can be used with "Marble Challenge" to determine the differences in time.

Math Activity 7.2: Mathematical Symbols

> **Difficulty Level:** Beginner
>
> **Objective:** Use mathematical symbols (greater than and less than) to interpret the results of an experiment
>
> **Supplies:** Copies of the activity sheet "Falling Objects" (Appendix D, page 182)

Interactive Dialogue

In the 7.1: On Your Mark, Get Set, Go!" investigation, we did an experiment to see which objects rolled down a ramp faster: a heavier object or a lighter object. Let's examine our results. We used "less than" (<) and "greater than" (>) signs in a previous experiment, so let's use them again.

If the time of the first object was not equal to the second object, was it greater than or less than? Let's record our results on the chart using the greater-than and less-than symbols in this manner.

The time of Object 1 was __________ (< or >) the time of Object 2.

Let's do the same with the other objects in our experiment.

Chapter 8

Gravity

Chapter Inquiry Question: How does gravity affect an object's motion?

Chapter Vocabulary/Word Wall: balance, gravity, decelerate

Inquire: Introductory Activity

Difficulty Level: Beginner

Objective: Establish the cause and effect of gravity's pull

Supplies: Small chair or stool

Introductory Activity 8.1: Newton's Apple

Interactive Dialogue

Think back on our experiment with falling objects. Objects may fall at the same time, but why do they fall at all? (Responses will vary.)

After Galileo, another scientist started observing falling objects as well. His name was Isaac Newton. It was said that he was once sitting in the garden when he saw an apple go plop! It fell right to the ground. He wondered, "Why did it fall straight down? Why not fall sideways, or why not pop off the tree and fly straight up in the air?"

Once he knew his problem, he then asked his question: Why do objects fall straight down to the ground?

And what comes after a question? (A hypothesis) *This is what he thought: There must be something inside of the Earth that pulls objects toward it.*

Now we have a name for that "something"—gravity. ***Gravity*** *is the force that pulls all physical objects, or objects that have mass, toward the Earth. All of us have mass, so we are all drawn to the Earth, like a piece of steel is drawn to a magnet. If not, we would float off into space.*

Discussion Points

- Why is the gravity in space very weak?
- What special problems related to gravity would an astronaut have in space?

Instruction

Discuss why gymnasts have to find their center of gravity to be able to **balance**, or distribute their weight equally, on a beam. Demonstrate the concept of a person's center of gravity: Place a chair or stool against a wall. Have a female student stand in front of the chair, legs spread slightly apart, and lean over forward with her back straight. Now, have her place her head against the wall and slowly bring the chair, or stool, up to her chest. Slowly, she should try to stand up straight, still holding the chair. Most girls will be able to do this since their center of gravity is lower; for boys, who have a higher center of gravity, this activity often proves to be more difficult.

Students can continue to explore the concept of center of gravity by finding the center of gravity of a ruler, a pencil, and other assorted objects by balancing them on one finger.

Inspire★

- Many books explore the world of gravity. Among them are these choice selections:
  - *Gravity All Around* by David Conrad
  - *How Do We Stay on Earth?* by Amy Henson
- The sounds of the fifties come alive in the Schoolhouse Rock video "Victim of Gravity," which is available on the Internet.
- Challenges and fun with weightlessness can be viewed from a directory of brief (12–15 second) clips on the NASA website. No sound is included, and you can select QuickTime or MPEG options.

Investigate: Science Activities

Science Activity 8.1: Egg Drop

Instruction

Remind the students that Galileo used a ramp to reduce the speed of a falling object enough so that he could determine its speed. Newton discovered that gravity pulls all objects to Earth.

In this experiment, students will work in teams to construct a nest for their egg. Their nest needs to serve like the ramp to **decelerate,** or slow down, the pull of gravity. They don't want their egg to break. How can they decelerate, or slow the acceleration to protect their egg?

Provide a set time limit for students to construct their nests. All nests should be dropped from the same height. (A ladder or an outdoor stairwell works well here.) Be sure to cover the area with plenty of large, plastic bags! Before the tests, students might like to draw a face on the egg—unless there is possibility of an emotional attachment!

Difficulty Level:
Advanced

Objective: Devise a structure that will **decelerate**, or slow down, the motion of a falling object to keep an egg from breaking when dropped

Supplies: (per team)
1 boiled or raw egg; 10 straws; three craft sticks; two sheets of paper towels; 1 shredded newspaper; plenty of large, plastic bags

Discussion Points

- How did your design help slow the speed of the falling nest?
- What was the strongest part of your nest?
- What was the weakest part of your nest?
- If you were going to make another nest, what changes would you make in your design?

Extension: Demonstrate the strength of an egg's natural design. Take a raw or boiled egg and ask students to predict what will happen if you stand it on end and push straight down. (Most students, knowing that eggs are fragile, will hypothesize that the egg will break.) Stand the egg on its end and press down. Discuss the results with students.

Difficulty Level: Beginner

Objective: Determine whether the size of a crater is affected when the object that creates the crater is dropped from various heights

Supplies: Pan half-filled with flour, marbles, ruler (or various coins) to measure the size of the crater, copies of the activity sheet "Impact! Measuring Craters" (Appendix D, page 184)

Science Activity 8.2: Impact!

Instruction

In this experiment, students will drop marbles from varying heights. Before dropping the marble from a given height, students should predict (using the size of the coins as a reference) how big the crater will be. Students should record their results on the "Impact! Measuring Craters" activity sheet. Following the activity, gather the class for a discussion of the results.

Integrate: ELA and Math Activities

Difficulty Level: Advanced

Objective: Create visual clues to help identify key science terms

Supplies: Unlined note cards, markers, pencils, pens, colored pencils, small envelopes, scissors

ELA Activity 8.1: Just Imagine!

Instruction

Students will be creating visual images to connect with vocabulary words in this unit. They will need to cut note cards in half. On one side of each card, they will write a vocabulary term; on the other side, they will draw an image that represents the word.

When the cards are complete, students will secure the envelope to a page in their Science Notebook and store their note cards inside. Possible words include the following, though others can be added.

gravity	mixture	acceleration
measure	record	height
solution	solid	mass

Math Activity 8.1: Equation and Balance

Instruction

Students have performed science activities that involve balance; math also involves balance. Explain that the equals sign in an equation means that the value on one side is the exact same value as another on the opposite side. Using connecting cubes (or sugar cubes), students will discover how various combinations of numbers can be used in simple equations. For instance, using ten cubes, students can create two different operations:

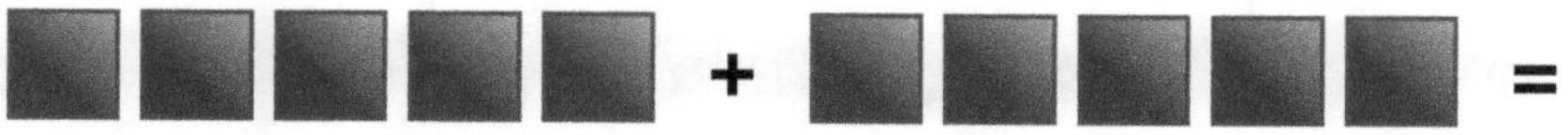

Both problems equal the number 10. Have students place 10 blocks after the equals signs in these equations to balance them.

Students can continue to explore other combinations of equations. To simplify, use fewer objects.

Difficulty Level: Advanced

Objective: Decompose numbers on both sides of an equation

Supplies: Balance, 20 assorted small objects for each student (e.g., tiles, paper clips)

Chapter 9

Motion, Force, and Energy

Chapter Inquiry Question: How do motion and force produce energy?

Chapter Vocabulary/Word Wall: energy, force, motion

Inquire: Introductory Activity

Difficulty Level: Beginner

Objective: Observe changes when force is applied to an object

Supplies: Ball

Introductory Activity 9.1: Get Energized!

Interactive Dialogue

Our scientist Isaac Newton had more than apples on his mind when he discovered that gravity keeps us all from floating away.

He had another important idea. He realized that if something is sitting still, it's just going to sit there until a force causes it to move. When something is in motion or moving, we say that there is ***movement****. I am going to place this ball on the table.*

- *What is happening?* (Nothing. It's not moving.)
- *How can I make it move?* (Push it.)

If I push it with my hand, I used force to cause it to move. ***Force*** *is the strength or energy that causes something to move. Let's talk more about energy.*

Have you ever said, "I just don't have any energy today"? If you lie on the couch, you may feel that way. You are lying still, so there's no motion. But energy is in your body. If you apply force by pushing away from the couch and stand up, the energy is present. ***Energy*** *is the ability to cause change—like pushing away from the couch and standing up!*

This time, let's move the ball with a different force. Now, I'm going to pull the ball toward me. That's a second kind of force, pulling. What was used when the ball was pulled backward? (Energy!)

Discussion Points

- What is energy?
- What are some other forces besides pushing and pulling that could move an object?

Instruction

Have a variety of objects ready for hands-on investigations. Students will pull and press objects in their search to find as many forces as possible. As each force is uncovered, have the student record it on a classroom chart. Some encouragement will be required to push or pull their thinking in the direction of the force that was used. Here are more examples:

Pull a wagon	*Pull* a book off a shelf
Push a toy car	*Twist* off a bottle cap
Squeeze toothpaste out of a tube	*Press* a doorbell
Wind a fishing reel	*Stretch* a rubber band

Inspire★

- Students will have plenty of fun as they identify the different kinds of forces demonstrated by familiar cartoon characters in the video "Soup or Sonic," which is available online. The video can be paused periodically to let students predict what will happen next.
- A more scientific explanation of force and motion can be seen in the video "Play Ball!—Motion & Forces," available on the 3-2-1 Contact website.
- Get ready to move with books that take movement to a whole new level:
  - *DO-4U the Robot Experiences Forces and Motion* by Mark Weakland
  - *Making Things Move* by Sian Smith
  - *Energy* by Christine Webster
  - *The Power of Energy* by Rebecca Weber

Investigate: Science Activities

Science Activity 9.1: Domino Trains

Instruction

Balance a domino on its end. Explain that, as discussed earlier (in the Interactive Dialogue), the domino will not be going anywhere unless something applies force that causes it to move. Push the domino over.

Next, set two dominoes on end, one in front of another. Bump one of the dominoes, demonstrating how the force causes both to topple.

Difficulty Level: Beginner

Objective: Demonstrate how speed and force work together

Supplies: Dominoes

Next, ask the students how placement of the dominoes might affect the results. What happens if dominoes are spaced close together? What if they are spaced farther apart? Allow students opportunities to form a hypothesis about various arrangements, such as "If the dominoes are far apart, they will fall at a faster speed than if they are closer together."

Group students in teams. Each team will need 20 dominoes. Teams will make two straight lines of dominoes with 10 dominoes in each line. One line will be spaced closely together; the other widely apart but still close enough so that each domino will push the next domino in line. Allow students to conduct this experiment several times with different variations.

Discussion Points

- What difference was observed between the two lines of dominoes?
- Was more force created by lining the dominoes closely together or wider apart?
- How did more force affect the speed of the falling dominoes?

Inspire★

An excellent explanation of the science behind falling dominoes can be seen on the video titled, "How many dominoes will topple a cathedral tower?" available on the Physics World website.

Investigate: Science Activities

Science Activity 9.2: The Need for Speed

Difficulty Level: Advanced

Objective: Discover how changes in surface texture can change the speed of an object

Supplies: Ramps of identical height (or materials for building ramps—e.g., cardboard, books, boards); various textures to lay over the ramps (e.g., carpet, aluminum foil, sandpaper, paper towel, waxed paper); toy cars of about the same size and weight; stopwatches; copies of the activity sheet "Speed and Surface Challenge" (Appendix D, page 185)

Instruction

Students will work in teams as they investigate the effect of different textures on the forward motion of a moving object. Teams will create their ramps and then form a hypothesis about which surface will allow the cars to move most quickly. Students will record their results on the "Speed and Surface Challenge" chart and add the chart to their Science Notebooks.

Integrate: ELA and Math Activities

ELA Activity 9.1: What Do You Know?

Instruction

Choose whether the class will research and write about Galileo or Newton. Review the chosen scientist, completing a KWL chart as you work. (This activity could also be conducted using an interactive board or three large sheets of chart paper—K, W, and L—taped to the wall.)

Ask the students to supply any information they already KNOW about the scientist. Write this information under "K."

Next, ask students to list additional details they WANT to know about the scientist your class is working with, and list questions under "W."

Now that they have a focus for their research, model the steps of the research process. Use books and the bookmarked Internet pages to find answers to the questions posed by students. Additional information that they LEARN will then be added to the class chart under "L."

Once enough information has been added, students will move to the next step. They will need to ask one very "big" question; big questions can be answered using some of the information that has been gathered; notes will be developed into a paragraph with different possible answers. Examples of big questions include the following:

- Why is he considered to be an important scientist?
- Why was he interested in science?

Students need to avoid "little" questions—those that have only one main answer. Examples of little questions include the following:

- Where did he go to school?
- When was he born?

Students should write down only the information they want to use to answer their big question. Next, they will decide how they want to arrange the information (the order of the facts). They will order the information by placing a number beside each fact they intend to use, beginning with the number 1.

To write their paragraphs, they will begin with a sentence that shows their big idea. Then they will complete the paragraph. Their last sentence will be a reflection sentence based on the information they have gathered. Example: He could have been a rich man, but he chose to be a scientist.

Difficulty Level: Advanced

Objective: Use prior knowledge and shared research to write an informative paragraph about a scientist

Supplies: Paper and pencils, books about Galileo or Newton, Internet bookmarks on Galileo or Newton pages; copies of the activity sheet "KWL Chart" (Appendix D, page 176)

Extension: Advanced students can complete a KWL chart for a scientist whom the class did not explore together and write a paragraph about that scientist.

Math Activity 9.1: Domino Math

Instruction

Students will work together in teams with a certain number of dominoes. Have them first turn the tiles facedown so that no dots are visible. When play begins, the first student will turn over two dominoes. That student must then count the dots to determine which domino has more dots. The team will confer to determine if the correct answer was given. Play continues for one complete round. Students can bump up the challenge by turning over three tiles the next round, then four tiles.

Difficulty Level: Beginner

Objective: Determine which domino has a greater number of dots

Supplies: Dominoes

Difficulty Level:
Advanced

Objective: Solve addition problems with dominoes

Supplies: Dominoes, copies of the activity sheet "Domino Math" (Appendix D, page 186)

Math Activity 9.2: Advanced Domino Math

Instruction

Distribute Domino Math sheets and a given number of dominoes to students. Students will place a domino faceup on the sheet with the largest number on the left. Then, they will write and solve addition or subtraction problems using the dots on the domino. For example, if one side of the domino has 6 dots and the other has 4, students might create the equation 6 + 4 = ____.

Extension: Challenge advanced students to perform the activity again, this time using subtraction or multiplication.

Chapter 10

Simple Machines

Chapter Inquiry Question: How do simple machines make work easier?

Chapter Vocabulary/Word Wall: inclined plane, lever, pulley, screw, simple machine, wedge, wheel and axle

Inquire: Introductory Activity

Introductory Activity 10.1: This Is a Job for . . . Simple Machines!

Difficulty: Beginner

Objective: Discover how work is made easier using simple machines

Supplies: Shoebox filled with small, heavy objects; thin board (or the ramp from earlier experiments); wooden wedge; small rug; copy of the "Simple Machine" poster (Appendix D, page 187)

Interactive Dialogue

I need your help. I have this very heavy box that I need to move from my desk to the other side of the room. I know you are all strong, but I don't want us to hurt ourselves, so we need to think of different ways we can move this box. Who has a good idea? (Responses will vary.)

Sounds like we need simple machines to do the work for us. What does the word simple mean? (Easy.) *A **simple machine** is a very easy tool. Earlier we learned that force can cause something to move. Some simple machines, like levers, help us multiply the force of our muscles, making it possible for us to lift something we could not lift without the machine. Other simple machines, like pulleys, change the direction of the force we apply; in other words, they change the direction of movement.*

Remember using a ramp in an earlier experiment? We moved balls and cars with our ramp. Let's set this ramp against the desk. Now, let's slide the box off of the desk onto the ramp. A little push, and there it goes. The ramp did the work for us.

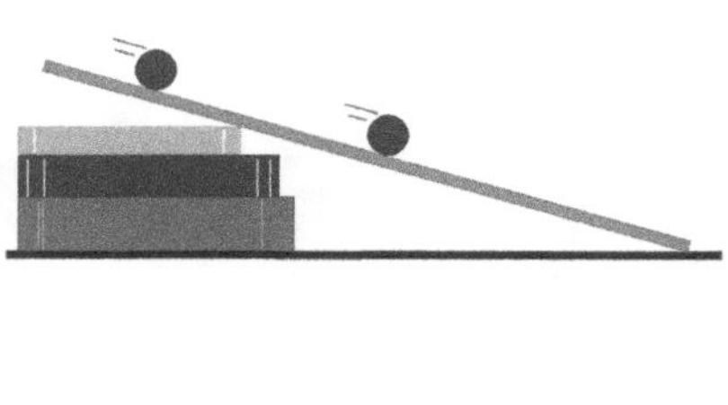

*The ramp is one example of a simple machine. Another name for a ramp is **inclined plane**. An incline is a slope, or angle, that we made by raising one end of the ramp. A plane is something that is flat, like our board.*

Now that we have the box on the floor, we need to move it to the other side of the room. We need a different simple machine. Let's use this pencil.

I am going to slip the point of the pencil just under the box. Then I will place a second pencil on the floor under the first pencil a small distance away from the box so that the two pencils make a t shape. When I push down on the pencil, what happens? (The pencil lifts the box.)

This is our second simple machine—a ***lever****. A lever is a bar or stick that can be used to move an object. The lever is now lifting the box. It is doing most of the work for us. We can slip this small rug under the end of the box now, remove the pencil, and pull the box across the room on the rug. Success!*

Discussion Points

- Why do we need simple machines?
- What other objects can a simple machine move? How?
- How is a slide on the playground a simple machine?

Instruction

Use the "Simple Machines" poster to show many ways that simple machines reduce the force needed for a task. Provide a mixed assortment of the following simple machines. Have students work together to sort them into the correct simple machine categories.

- **Lever**: stapler, scissors, bottle opener
- **Wheel and axle**: doorknob, fishing rod
- **Screw**: pencil sharpener, bottle cap
- **Wedge**: hammer, fork, doorstop
- **Inclined Plane**: ramp, ladder
- **Pulley**: sails on a ship, window blinds (items with pulleys)

Flip Foldable

Step 1: Give 3 sheets of construction paper to each pair of students.

Step 2: Students cut all 3 sheets in half lengthwise. Each student gets half the stack.

Step 3: Stagger the sheets so that the end of each one peeps out from below the one in front of it.

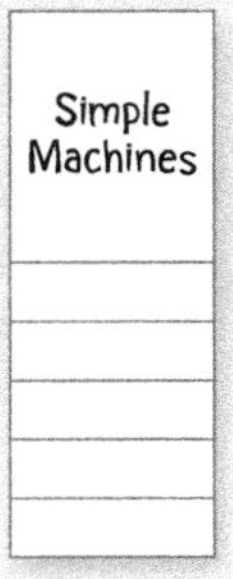

Step 4: Holding the stack firmly, students will bend the stack backward, lining it up so that 6 roughly equal "tabs" (including the top one) descend down the entire length of the foldable.

Following the discussion, students will create a Simple Machine flip foldable as shown in the diagram. Students will label each of the tabs with the name of a simple machine. Then, they will open the foldable to that "page" and, above the label, make a drawing of a machine that fits in the category.

Inspire★

- A fun explanation of the science behind a catapult can be found in Bill Nye's "Simple Machines" video, which provides several examples. This short video can be found on the Internet.
- The Chicago Museum of Science and Industry hosts an online activity that provides an excellent demonstration of simple machines using a lazy character looking for easier ways to do his job. This makes an exciting class activity, with students providing ideas for parts the character needs to build the machines.
- Go back in time with *Lance Dragon in Lance Dragon Defends His Castle with Simple Machines* by Eric Braun.
- Explore the six-book series *Simple Machines to the Rescue* by Sharon Thales.

Investigate: Science Activities

Science Activity 10.1: Cotton Ball Catapult

Instruction

Get in on the fun! Model the process of creating a catapult as students follow the steps.

Step 1: Stack three craft sticks on top of each other.

Step 2: Get two more sticks. Place one of them under the stack and one on top of the stack, so that the two sticks (which are in line with one another) form a t shape with the stack of three sticks.

Step 3: Place a spoon on the top stick, with the bowl side facing up, and the length of the spoon and stick are fully in line. Use a rubber band to secure the ends of the two sticks and the end of the spoon together. The space between the two sticks (caused by the space taken up by the three sticks in between) will provide tension. (Adjust the rubber band as necessary to create the tension.)

Step 4: The cotton ball goes into the bowl of the spoon. The spoon is pulled back lightly and then released, sending the cotton ball flying.

Difficulty Level: Beginner

Objective: Create a lever (a simple machine) that will demonstrate transfer of energy

Supplies: Craft sticks, cotton balls, rubber bands, plastic spoons

Extension: This activity can easily be made more advanced by dividing the class into teams and allowing them to design their own catapults from a wide assortment of materials (e.g., boxes, paper tubes, straws, tape, and small interlocking blocks). Teams can compete to see whose catapult will launch a Ping-Pong ball the greatest distance.

Difficulty Level: Advanced

Objective: Demonstrate transfer of energy using a pulley

Supplies: Variety of spools (e.g., from fishing line or ribbons), pencils or straws, long pieces of string, flags made with paper and markers

Science Activity 10.2: Raise the Flag

Instruction

This project can be performed in pairs or (if spools are in short supply) teams. Discuss the problem people once encountered in trying to lower or raise a flag on a pole. A ladder (i.e., an inclined plane) could be used, but another simple machine—a pulley—made climbing up a ladder unnecessary. Problem solved!

For this investigation, divide the class into teams so students discover how a pulley system works.

Step 1: Flags are created with images of students' own choosing. (Creativity rules!)

Step 2: Run the pencil through the spool so that the spool can spin.

Step 3: Tie the ends of a string together to make a long loop.

Step 4: Tape one end of the flag to the bottom of the string.

Step 5: Loop the string over the spool, with string on both sides of the spool. While one student holds the ends of the pencil, another student pulls down on the string opposite to the flag, moving the flag upward.

Following the activity, gather students for a discussion. Explain that the pulley changes the direction of the force. (Pulling down on the string makes the flag go up.)

Discussion Point

- How would a pulley help someone who wanted to get water from a well?

Difficulty Level: Advanced

Objective: Identify simple machines

Supplies: "Soup or Sonic" video used in previous chapter

Science Activity 10.3: Name That Simple Machine

Interactive Dialogue

In the previous chapter, forces and motion were the focus while the class viewed "Soup or Sonic." Now it's time to bump it up a notch! This time as we watch, we will try to identify the simple machines that the characters use.

Instruction

View the video again, pausing as appropriate to discuss the simple machines that appear on the screen.

Integrate: ELA and Math Activities

Difficulty Level: Advanced

Objective: Create a piece of narrative writing

Supplies: Pencils and paper

ELA Activity 10.1: The Twiddles

Interactive Dialogue

Oh no! The Twiddle family needs your help. The Twiddles are tiny creatures who live in a small hole in a Gabnut tree. During a big storm, a lightning bolt split the tree wide open. The stairs to climb down the tree are on one

side, but the family is on the other side. You are to write the ending of this story. How will they get down? Remember that their home is filled with many strange objects. They will need to use at least two simple machines to help them escape and land safely on the ground.

Math Activity 10.1: Cotton Ball Math

Difficulty Level: Advanced

Objective: Represent addition and subtraction functions using cotton balls

Supplies: Cotton balls, copies of the activity sheet "Cotton Ball Math" (Appendix D, page 188)

Instruction

Give a "Cotton Ball Math" chart and 10 cotton balls to each student. They will use the activity sheet for support as they solve basic addition and subtraction problems.

Chapter 11

Magnetic Attraction

Chapter Inquiry Question: How is Earth like a magnet?

Chapter Vocabulary/Word Wall: attract, magnet, repel

Inquire: Introductory Activity

Difficulty Level: Advanced

Objective: Demonstrate the properties of a magnet

Supplies: Flat magnets, pans filled with metal and nonmetal objects (e.g., paper clips, nails, rubber bands, buttons, twist ties, small metal cars); globe; copies of the activity sheet "Magnetic Attraction" (Appendix D, page 189)

Introductory Activity 11.1: It's Magnetic!

Interactive Dialogue

We know that we can see the results of forces that push or pull, stretch or press, but there's still another kind of force. This force is completely invisible. It's called a magnetic field.

A ***magnet*** *is a special kind of metal that has an invisible force around it that* ***attracts****, or pulls, metal. For example, the metal found in this paper clip or this nail would be attracted to a magnet.*

But the magnet doesn't pick up this rubber band or this penny. Why is that? (Responses will vary.) *The penny is made of other types of metal, ones that are not attracted to magnets, and the rubber band is not made of metal at all.*

Now watch as I move this magnet toward the car. What happened? (The car moved.) *We know that there is a force because the car moved. It was attracted to the magnet by the magnet's magnetic force.*

You can amaze your friends with some magic using a magnet. Watch this demonstration. Simply hold a magnet under a table. Have a metal object on top of the table, like these paper clips. Then, move the magnet around until the objects are caught in the magnet's force field, and then what happens? (The objects move around!) *It's like magic!*

Do you know that there is metal deep, deep inside the Earth? That metal makes Earth one giant magnet with its own force field. The Earth, like this bar magnet, has a north pole and a south pole. The North Pole is on top of this globe, and the South Pole is on bottom.

Notice what happens when I try to push together the south poles of these two magnets. What happens? (The poles push each other away.) *They* ***repel*** *each other, or push away from each other. Now let's flip one of these around so its north pole is heading toward the other magnet's south pole. What do you think will happen now?* (The magnets will attract each other.) *Opposite poles, or one north pole and one south pole, will attract each other. Opposites attract!*

Discussion Points

- Why are some objects attracted to magnets but others are not?
- How is Earth like a magnet?

Instruction

In this activity teams will test their magnets using an assortment of objects gathered into a bucket. Then they will complete the two-column activity sheet titled "Magnetic Attraction" and add it to their Science Notebooks.

Inspire★

- The magnet song "Magnets," available online at Teacher Tube, musically demonstrates the properties of a magnet.
- Books to extend students' investigation into this popular topic include:
    - *Magnets* by Angela Royston
    - *Magnets Push, Magnets Pull* by Mark Weakland
- SmartBoard fans will enjoy the magnet units available on the Smart Tech website.

Investigate: Science Activities

Science Activity 11.1: Sandbox Discovery

Instruction

Students will excavate a sandpit as they search for objects attracted to magnets. When they run their magnets over the sand, metal objects will pop to the surface.

Discussion Points

- Why were some objects attracted to the magnet and others not?

Difficulty Level: Beginner

Objective: Distinguish between things that are attracted to magnets and those that are not attracted to them

Supplies: Magnets, assorted metal and nonmetal objects buried in a sand-filled pan (e.g., paper clips, nails, rubber bands, buttons, twist ties, small metal cars)

Difficulty Level: Advanced

Objective: Demonstrate the presence of a magnetic field

Supplies: Horseshoe magnets, paper clips, tape, string, markers, small pieces of paper cut into diamond shapes about 3 inches (7.62 cm) long

Science Activity 11.2: Go Fly a Kite!

Instruction

Step 1: Students use the diamond-shaped pieces of paper to create kites illustrated with images showing their own interests.

Step 2: Tape the paper clip to one end of the kite.

Step 3: Tape one end of the string to the other end of the kite.

Step 4: Tape the loose end of the string to a table.

Step 5: Pick up the kite and aim the magnet in its direction (but don't touch it with the magnet). This will allow the magnet's field to take over.

Step 6: Release the kite and watch it fly!

Discussion Points

- How did the experiment successfully show the presence of a magnetic field?
- What work did the magnet do?

Integrate: ELA and Math Activities

Difficulty Level: Beginner

Objective: Spell vocabulary words encountered in the Physical Science unit, with Science Notebooks as a guide

Supplies: Cookie sheets, magnetic letters

ELA Activity 11.1: Spill and Spell

Instruction

In small groups, students will refer to their Science Notebooks to find important terms from the Physical Science unit. Then they will spell the words on the cookie sheet (magnetic only) using magnetic letters.

This activity can be made into a game that students play in pairs: One student begins spelling the word and another student tries to guess the word before the last letter is attached to the board.

Math Activity 11.1: Fishing for Math with Magnets

Instruction

Step 1: Scatter magnetic numbers face-down.

Step 2: Tie one end of the string to a pencil and the other to a magnet.

Step 3: Small groups of students "go fishing" for numbers.

Step 4: After a student catches two numbers, he or she will write them on the first fish on their "Fishing for Math" activity sheet.

Step 5: Students return their numbers to the fishing hole and fish for two more numbers (for the next fish) and continue until each fish on the "Fishing for Math" sheet has an equation for them to complete.

Difficulty Level: Advanced

Objective: Combine randomly "caught" numbers to create addition problems

Supplies: Magnetic numbers, magnets, string, pencils, copies of the activity sheet "Fishing for Math" (Appendix D, page 190)

Extension: Students "fish" for five numbers and then arrange them from low to high.

Name: ____

Unit 2 Assessment (b)

Circle the correct answer.

1. When an ice cube melts, it becomes a _________.
   a. liquid
   b. gas
   c. solid
   d. simple machine
2. Objects that accelerate _________.
   a. move more quickly
   b. move more slowly
   c. change direction
   d. stop
3. Objects fall to the ground because of _________.
   a. properties of matter
   b. simple machines
   c. gravity
   d. motion
4. Draw things that show the three states of matter.

5. How does a magnet work? Write or draw your answer.

©2014 Kaye Hagler from *Inquire, Investigate, Integrate*. This page may be reproduced for classroom use only.

Name: ____

Unit 2 Assessment (a)

Multiple Choice: Select the letter that best answers each problem.

1. A __________ is a state of matter that has a definite shape.

a. liquid

b. solid

c. organism

d. gas

2. When a solid melts, what does it become?

a. another solid

b. a gas

c. ice

d. a liquid

3. Which of the following is NOT a property of a liquid?

a. It takes the shape of its container.

b. It is invisible.

c. It has weight/mass.

d. It can be measured.

4. What is the sequence of events for the changing state of an ice cube?

a. solid, gas, liquid

b. liquid, gas, solid

c. solid, liquid, gas

d. gas, solid, liquid

5. Objects go down when they fall because of __________.

a. motion

b. a magnetic force

c. gravity

d. acceleration

Dig-Deeper Questions:

6. You have been asked to help prepare lunch. These are the materials you have found in the kitchen:

lemons	salt	apple slices	raisins	mayonnaise	water
sugar	bananas	peanut butter	limes	peanuts	bread

A. From the list, circle three items you would use to create a mixture.

B. From this same list of materials, underline three items you would use to create a solution.

©2014 Kaye Hagler from *Inquire, Investigate, Integrate*. This page may be reproduced for classroom use only.

7. On a hike through the woods, you suddenly stumble. Your very heavy bug book and your baseball cap fly over a cliff. Which will most likely occur?

   a. The book will land first.

   b. The cap will land first.

   c. They should land at the same time.

8. A soccer ball is flying through the air toward the goal. You are on the opposing team. Describe two different forces that could be used to keep the other team from scoring that goal.

   a. ____________________

   b. ____________________

9. As you ride your bike, you hit a bump. A metal screw goes flying off your bike and lands under a metal grate. You reach down and try to get it, but it is just out of reach. How can you get the screw?

   ____

   ____

   ____

Scientific Inquiry Problem

10. You and a friend are on a hike. Along the way, you discover a large dinosaur bone sticking out of the dirt. The two of you want to take it home, but you have to cross a creek to get there. How can you remove the bone from the dirt and cross the creek using at least two simple machines?

   a. Name the first simple machine. ____________________

   ____

   b. How would you use it? ____________________

   ____

   c. Name the second simple machine. ____________________

   ____

   d. How would you use it? ____________________

   ____

 ©2014 Kaye Hagler from *Inquire, Investigate, Integrate*. This page may be reproduced for classroom use only.

Unit 3

Earth and Space Science

Chapter 12

Patterns of the Earth, Moon, and Sun

Chapter Inquiry Question: How do the movements of the Earth, moon, and sun represent a pattern?

Chapter Vocabulary/Word Wall: pattern, phases, rotation

Inquire: Introductory Activity

Difficulty Level: Beginner

Objective: Discover the patterns of rotation created by the Earth, moon, and sun

Supplies: Flashlight, globe (or ball)

Introductory Activity 12.1: Day After Day: Natural Patterns in Space

Interactive Dialogue

When you step outside on a clear morning, what brightens the sky? (sun)

What happens to the sun at night? (it seems to set, go down)

Does this happen over and over again? (yes)

When something is repeated in the same way over and over again, we call that a ***pattern****. Another example is brushing your teeth every night. That's a pattern. The Earth has its own pattern. It turns around and around. We call the round-and-round movement* ***rotation****. As Earth turns, it also moves around and around the sun. It's as simple as night and day! Watch and let's see how this works.*

I need someone to hold the flashlight—you will be the sun. Next, I need someone to hold this globe (or ball). You will be the Earth. Sun, you shine your light directly on Earth. Earth, very slowly rotate the globe you are holding in your hands. Keep it moving around and around from side to side. As you rotate, move slowly around the sun, toward your right hand.

Sun, your job is to keep your light pointed at the Earth. Let's turn out the lights so that we can see this pattern better, and let's make a large area for our Earth and Sun to move. Notice how the side away from the sun is

dark. That is because it is night on that side, but what is happening on the side now facing the sun? (daytime.) *Good job!* (Turn the lights back on.)

OK, so the Earth rotates as it goes around the sun, but while the Earth is going around the sun, another object is moving around the Earth. It is very visible at night. What is that object? (the moon)

The moon has its own pattern. If you observe the moon one night, it might be just a small sliver. Remember our word fraction*? Sometimes we can only see a fraction, or what looks like a broken piece, of the moon. But after the moon gets about as small as it can, then it starts slowly getting bigger and brighter. Finally, one clear night, a very bright, whole moon appears in the sky. We call that a full moon! The moon's pattern—big-then-small-then big-again—is called the* ***phases*** *of the moon.*

All of these patterns of sun, Earth, and moon are natural processes!

Discussion Points

- The patterns of the sun, Earth, and moon work together naturally. But how are these patterns like a machine?
- What are other patterns, or things that are repeated over and over again, in nature?

Inspire★

- An excellent description and short video animation of the changing phases of the moon, titled "Phases of the Moon," is available on the History Channel's website.
- Another video depicting the phases of the moon is available on NASA's website: "Phases of the Moon Animation."
- Charlotte Guillain's six-book series *Space* provides easy-to-follow descriptions and visual illustrations, including books titled, *The Sun, The Moon, Stars, Planets, Earth,* and *Astronauts.*
- Fiction texts related to this chapter's content include the following:
  - *Eye to Eye* by Scott McCloud
  - *Blastoff to the Secret Side of the Moon* by Scott Nickel

Investigate: Science Activities

Science Activity 12.1: Gravity and Earth's Rotation

Difficulty Level: Beginner

Objective: Demonstrate the pull of the sun's gravity

Supplies: Large area for movement; small signs, each labeled with one month of the year; calendar

Instruction

Step 1: Assign one student to be the sun, one to be the Earth.

Step 2: Give 12 students a different sign (pieces of paper, each with a different month's name). While they stand in a circle, students should be arranged in sequential order from January to December.

Step 3: Position the sun and Earth in the middle of the circle.

Step 4: The students with the month signs should hold them with one hand and hold their other hand outstretched toward the Earth.

Step 5: Adjust the size of the circle so that students' outstretched hands are just out of reach of the Earth, and the Earth has room to rotate around the sun.

Step 6: Very slowly, the sun pulls the Earth in a counterclockwise direction, going around in a circle. While the Earth is rotating with the sun, it should reach out to the other students, trying to tap hands.

Step 7: Once the Earth has passed all 12 "months," explain that one year has passed. It takes one full year for the Earth to revolve around the sun.

After the activity, remind students about gravity—that it pulls two objects toward each other. Since the sun is larger than the Earth, the sun's gravity is stronger. The Earth can't pull away and go in any other direction because the sun's gravity holds it in place.

Discussion Points

- How does the sun keep the Earth from flying all over outer space?
- After examining a calendar, have a volunteer provide a hypothetical guess as to the months when the Earth is closer to the sun and the months when the Earth is farther away.
- Are calendars based on man-made events or natural events? Why?
- Is the Earth close to the sun on your birthday or farther away? What kinds of activities can the guests at your birthday party play?

Extension: Conduct the same activity as above, but this time add the moon. (Widen the circle as necessary.) The moon holds onto the hand of Earth and rotates around Earth, but they release hands halfway around each turn and clasp again on the other side. Explain that it takes the moon approximately 1 month to rotate around the Earth.

Difficulty Level: Advanced

Objective: Visualize the rotation of the moon around Earth

Supplies: Blue and gray construction paper, scissors, dark marker

Science Activity 12.2: The Moon's Rotation Around Earth

Instruction

Students cut out a blue circle (Earth) and a smaller gray circle (the moon). Using a marker, students make one small dot near the edge of the gray circle. The mark is a crater. Lay the circles flat on a table.

Have the students rotate the moon counterclockwise around the Earth so that the crater is always nearest Earth. This will demonstrate the rotation of the moon around Earth.

After the experiment, have students glue the circles into their Science Notebooks and label the page "Rotation of the Earth and Moon."

Discussion Points

- How does gravity work in this natural process (or system)?
- How is the rotation of the Earth and moon different from the rotation of hands on a clock?

Science Activity 12.3: Sundial

Difficulty Level: Beginner

Objective: Track the changing position of the sun

Supplies: Paper plate, straw, pencils, markers, watch, small pebbles, rulers

Instruction

This experiment will require several sunny days. Students can work as a class or individually. The first task should be done before noon. Punch a hole in the middle of the plate with the pencil. Insert the straw.

Go outside and find a sunny spot somewhat off the beaten track. Use the pebbles or some other weights to keep the plate from blowing away. Watch the time carefully. At noon, observe where the pencil's shadow falls. With the marker, write the number 12 near the edge of this shadow.

Continue to mark the plate hourly according to the position of the shadow (1:00, 2:00, etc.). The next day, add more numbers according to the position of the shadow.

Use the ruler to measure the approximate distance between the numbers. This measurement will allow students to complete the clock face with the remaining numbers. Check the device several times over the next few days to see how accurately it keeps time.

Discussion Points

- Why did the shadows keep moving around the plate from one hour to the next? Would this be an accurate way to tell time?
- In the coming weeks and months, these shadows will no longer match the numbers but will keep moving. Why will the shadows change positions?

Integrate: ELA and Math Activities

ELA Activity 12.1: The Man in the Moon

Difficulty Level: Advanced

Objective: Create a piece of descriptive writing

Supplies: Pencils, copies of the activity sheet "The Man in the Moon" (Appendix D, page 191)

Instruction

Explain to the students that some people think a face can be seen on a full moon. They call him the "The Man in the Moon."

Have students draw a circle on the page and a man's face in the moon. Then, they will write a story about how the man became trapped in the moon. Before they write their story, they will enjoy listening to the song "Hey, Hey, Mr. Moon" or watching the animated video of the same title; both are available online.

Difficulty Level:
Beginner

Objective: Use addition and subtraction to solve fact families

Supplies: Pencils, copies of the activity sheet "Fly to the Moon" (Appendix D, page 192)

Math Activity 12.1: Fly to the Moon

Instruction

Students will complete math problems as their rocket ship moves toward the moon. Remind them that they must answer problems in the correct sequence before they can advance.

Chapter 13

Properties of the Sun

Chapter Inquiry Question: How does the sun provide energy for the Earth?

Chapter Vocabulary/Word Wall: air pollution, solar, solar system

Inquire: Introductory Activity

Introductory Activity 13.1: Heat Wave!

Difficulty Level: Beginner

Objective: Determine the impact of the sun's energy on the Earth

Supplies: Picture of the sun

Interactive Dialogue

Why do we wear hats and sunglasses? (to protect us from the sun) *Why do we squirt sunscreen onto our skin in the summer?* (to protect us from the sun) *Why do we put up large umbrellas when we go to the beach?* (to protect us from the sun)

The temperature in this room is about 72 degrees. What would happen if I turned it up to 100 degrees? (We would get very hot.) *What if I turned it up to 1,000 degrees?* (We would die.) *What about 10,000 degrees?* (We might dry up!)

That's the temperature you would find on the sun—10,000 degrees. When you light a fire, the flaming, hot gas can burn you if you touch it. That's exactly what the sun is made of—flaming hot gases. That's why no one could live on this giant star.

In fact, the sun is the star at the center of our solar system. Remember that a system is a group of things work together. ***Solar*** *is a word we use to describe something about the sun. For example, solar energy is energy that comes from the sun. The* ***solar system*** *is the system of objects—including Earth, other planets, and moons—that all move around the sun. The sun is so powerful that it is our main source of energy. Its power gives us light and heat. It causes plants to grow. It controls the weather and the seasons.*

Discussion Points

- If plants need the energy given by the sun to grow, what happens to that energy if we eat the plants?
- Why is the sun the center of our solar system?

Inspire★

- Important facts about the sun are clearly animated for students in the video "Super Sun."
- Images from NASA provide a small glimpse of the burning gases that releases the sun's energy.
- The Canadian Dermatology Association's "Sun Safe Play Everyday!" combines interesting facts about the sun with important information on the effects of too much sun.
- The power of the sun is brought to light in a wide range of informational/nonfiction texts, including the following:
    - *Sunlight* by Sue Barraclough
    - *Sunlight* by Erin Edison
    - *Sunshine* by Gail Saunders-Smith
    - *The Power of Energy* by Rebecca Weber

Investigate: Science Activities

Science Activity 13.1: The Power of the Sun

Difficulty Level: Beginner

Objective: Observe the visible effect of the sun by simulating the skin's exposure to too much sunlight

Supplies: Sunscreen, dark construction paper, copies of the activity sheet "Power of the Sun" (Appendix D, page 193)

Instruction

Have students fold a sheet of construction paper in half. On one side, they will lightly smear the sunscreen, being careful to not cross the fold line. Tape the paper to a very sunny window or take it outside and secure it in a sunny spot. In their Science Notebooks, students can use the "Power of the Sun" activity sheet; below the heading they should describe (or draw) the setup of the experiment. They will then predict what will happen. After the experiment, they can write (or draw) the actual results.

Discussion Points

- How were the two sides of the paper different in color?
- Why was one side darker than the other?
- How does this prove the need for wearing sunscreen when we are going to be outside on a sunny day?

Science Activity 13.2: Melting Ice

Instruction

Explain that just as people need to be protected from the strong rays of the sun, the Earth also needs protection. Too much sun can cause crops to die, rivers and streams to dry up, and glaciers to melt. In this experiment, students use ice cubes to explore several ways to minimize the power of the sun.

Students will use the available materials to create a shield for the ice cube in order to protect it and slow the melting time. Some students may choose to build structures that cover the entire glass, while others may simply cover the top. After all shields have been completed, place one ice cube into each cup and cover the cup with a shield. Students should place their cups in the warmest spot in the classroom, preferably near a window, and record the start time on the "Melting Ice" activity sheet. They will continue to monitor their ice every 10 minutes and make a brief description on their charts. They will continue to record their results until the ice has completely melted.

Discussion Points

- What types of shields worked best? Why?
- What kind of shields offered the least protection for the ice? Why?

Difficulty Level: Beginner

Objective: Create a container that slows the effects of the sun's heat

Supplies: Clear plastic cups; ice cubes; tape; scissors; timer; various materials to block the sun (e.g., aluminum foil, plastic, thin cardboard, plain white paper, cardboard); copies of the activity sheet "Melting Ice" (Appendix D, page 194)

Integrate: ELA and Math Activities

ELA Activity 13.1: It's in the Air

Difficulty Level: Advanced

Objective: Write a cause–effect paragraph

Supplies: Paper and pencils

Interactive Dialogue

If you sit in a car on a summer day with the windows rolled up, what begins to happen? (You get hot.) *The windows let the heat into the car, but they do not let it out. To get rid of the heat, we have to open the windows.*

Now imagine a layer of gas covering the entire Earth. This layer protects Earth from the intense heat of the sun. That's a good thing. But every time we burn trees and forests or drive cars that burn a whole lot of gas or use electricity for hours and hours, we damage the layer of gas that is supposed to protect us from the sun. That's not good.

Every time we throw away bags and bags of garbage, our landfills grow bigger and bigger. Sometimes we burn garbage, and that also damages our protective layer.

Because of things that humans do, the Earth's protective layer is being damaged more and more. Earth is getting hotter and hotter.

We call the damaging gases that humans create (and that damage our protective layer) air pollution. What are some different ways that air pollution hurts us and our planet? (Responses will vary but may include making it difficult to breathe, changing the climate, etc.)

Instruction

Before beginning this writing assignment, review causes of air pollution and its effects.

Students will complete a two-column chart showing the causes of air pollution and the effects of air pollution. They will use this information to write a cause–effect paragraph on air pollution. Work as a whole group if your students need additional support.

Inspire★

Consider reading *Polluted Air* by Angela Royston to further explore air pollution with your students.

Difficulty Level: Advanced

Objective: Create a pie chart

Supplies: Colored pencils and paper, copies of the activity sheet "Air Pollution Pie Chart" (Appendix D, page 195)

Math Activity 13.1: Air Pollution Pie Chart

Instruction

Review the data below with students to share with them the most common causes of air pollution. Then have them color the slices in the pie chart to represent major contributors to air pollution.

- 50% cars, trucks and other transportation (Students color 5 slices blue.)
- 30% factories (Students color 3 slices red.)
- 20% homes and businesses (Students color 2 "slices" yellow.)

Discussion Points

- According to the pie charts, what causes the most air pollution?
- How can the biggest source of air pollution be controlled?
- What source of air pollution causes the least amount? How can this number be reduced?

After students complete the work, they should add their pie charts to their Science Notebooks.

Chapter 14

The Water Cycle

Chapter Inquiry Question: What is the water cycle and how does it work?

Chapter Vocabulary/Word Wall: atmosphere, cloud, condensation, evaporation, water cycle, weather

Inquire: Introductory Activity

Introductory Activity 14.1: Today's Weather Forecast

Difficulty Level: Beginner (with Advanced Variation)

Objective: Explain the process of the water cycle

Supplies: Science Notebook, copies of the activity sheet "Water Cycle" (Appendix D, page 196)

Interactive Dialogue

If I look up into the sky and see big, dark clouds, what should I grab before I leave home? A raincoat or a swimsuit? (raincoat) *A bottle of water or an umbrella?* (umbrella) *Why?* (It will probably rain.) *If I look up and see clear blue skies, can I go outside and play?* (yes) *Why?* (It probably won't rain.)

If I want to know what kind of day it is going to be, but it's still dark outside, what can I do? (Watch a weather report on TV or the Internet.)

If it is summer, what kind of weather can I expect? (hot, sunny)

If it is winter, what kind of weather can I expect? (snow, cold)

So what is weather? (Responses will vary but will probably include examples like sunshine, rain, etc.)

***Weather** is the word used to describe the way air behaves up in the atmosphere (or high in the sky). It includes the temperature (or how hot or cold it is), the wetness or dryness, and the degree of cloudiness and sunshine. The **atmosphere** is the layer of gas that covers the Earth, which we talked about earlier. Weather is another natural process because it happens naturally. People don't create the weather.*

*When the sun's energy beams down on rivers, seas, and oceans, some of the water disappears into the air as water vapor, a gas. This change from liquid to gas is called **evaporation**. When this gas goes way up into the sky,* *it begins to form tiny droplets of liquid. We call the change from gas to liquid* ***condensation****.*

We can see condensation in the sky: clouds! A ***cloud*** *is formed when water vapor turns back into liquid, forming droplets. When the water droplets get all crushed together, the liquid begins spilling out. What do we call that?* (rain) *It could be rain or sleet or snow.*

All of these times that moisture falls from the sky, we have precipitation—a really big word. After the rain hits mountains or hills or riverbanks, where does it go? (It flows to streams, rivers, ponds, oceans.) *So once the water is back on the surface of Earth, the sun zaps it again, and what happens?* (Responses will vary.) *The cycle starts all over again, and the liquid water can turn to a solid (ice) or a gas (water vapor). We call that the* ***water cycle****—the movement of water from land to air, then back again.*

Extension: Paste pictures of different kinds of clouds (cumulus, cirrus, and stratus) to sheets of cardstock. Then add craft-stick handles. On cloudy days, students can match the pictures to the clouds in the sky.

Discussion Points

- How does the sun affect the weather?
- What can happen when too much rain falls on a particular area?
- What factors could disrupt, or interfere with, the regular patterns of the water cycle?

Instruction

Students will create a diagram of the water cycle in their Science Notebook using the activity sheet "Water Cycle." First, they will draw a body of water, land formations, clouds, and the sun. Next, they will create labels for each part of the process—Evaporation, Condensation, and Precipitation—with arrows to show the sequential steps of the cycle. (For less advanced students, simpler labels—water, sun, cloud, rain/snow—can be used.)

Inspire★

- Students of all ages will love the rap that musically explains the water cycle in the video "Water Cycle Jump." Many versions of this rap are available on the Internet, and students will find themselves chanting along: "Rain! Rain!"
- An animated explanation of the water cycle can be found on the Internet in a video by the Community Collaborative Rain, Hail and Snow Network. The video is titled "The Water Cycle."
- On a more advanced level, students will be awed by the visual effects of the water cycle in a video titled "Earth Water Cycle," which is provided online by NASA.

- Supplemental resources for the study of the water cycle include the following books:
  - *The Water Cycle* by Craig Hammersmith
  - *Water Basics* by Carol K. Lindeen
  - *The Water Cycle* by Rebecca Olien

Extension: "Water Cycle! Water Cycle!" Divide students into teams of four. Each group will operate as one of the following weather stations: Water, Vapor, Cloud, or Rain. (As appropriate for your students, you may choose more advanced terms: Ground Water Evaporation, Condensation, Precipitation).

With a leader prompting the calls, teams will shout at the same time "Water Cycle! Water Cycle!" At that point, teams run to the next station in the cycle. When they land in their new station, they all yell out their station's name. Once all teams are in place again, the leader begins the chant again, "Water Cycle! Water Cycle!" and students continue to the next station.

Continue the game in this fashion until teams return to their first station.

Investigate: Science Activities

Science Activity 14.1: Bottled Water

Instruction

Students will work in teams. First, each team will pick a name and write it on the bottom of its bottle with a marker. Then they will follow these steps:

Step 1: Students fill the bottle about three-fourths full of water.

Step 2: Students draw a line on the bottle to mark the water level and write the date and temperature.

Step 3: The bottles are placed in a sunny location.

Step 4: Students monitor their experiment periodically for a week, recording data (i.e., the water level, the date, and the temperature) on their bottles, as in Step 2 above.

Discussion Points

- What did students observe happening to the water in their bottles?
- How did temperature affect the rate of evaporation?

Difficulty Level: Advanced

Objective: Demonstrate the connection between temperature and water evaporation

Supplies: Clear plastic bottles with the top of the necks removed (or tall glass containers), permanent markers, thermometers

Difficulty Level: Beginner

Objective: Observe the process of condensation, or "cloud making"

Supplies: Clear, plastic cups; warm water; masking tape

Science Activity 14.2: Clouds in a Cup

Instruction

Step 1: Give two plastic cups to each student or each small group.

Step 2: Pour a small amount of warm water into one cup.

Step 3: Have the students immediately turn the second cup upside down and tape it to the first cup.

Step 4: Students should closely observe the sides of their cups. They will observe the sides of the first cup and then the second becoming cloudy.

Step 5: After the sides of both cups have completely clouded over, have the students separate the cups and run their fingers through the moisture that has condensed inside the top cup.

Discussion Points

- What was observed during the experiment?
- Why did the second cup become cloudy?
- How does this experiment show part of the water cycle?

Difficulty Level: Beginner

Objective: Simulate clouds and the process of precipitation

Supplies: Clear, plastic cups; water; shaving cream; blue food coloring

Science Activity 14.3: Rain Clouds

Instruction

Step 1: Students fill their cups approximately three-fourths full of water.

Step 2: Students squirt a "cloud" of shaving cream on top of the water.

Step 3: Students place a few drops of food coloring in only one spot on their cloud.

Step 4: Students observe as the shaving cream (the cloud) becomes saturated with the extra moisture until finally it rains!

Discussion Point

- How did the shaving cream and food coloring show one step in the water cycle?

Integrate: ELA and Math Activities

Difficulty Level: Beginner

Objective: Explore homophones

Supplies: Pencils, copies of the activity sheet "Homophones" (Appendix D, page 197)

ELA Activity 14.1: Letter Drop

Instruction

Using the activity sheet, students will use words from this chapter to explore the concept of homophones. First, they will fill in the missing letters to make words. Then, they will draw the picture that goes with each word.

This lesson can be expanded using other homophones, including flower/flour, night/knight, toes/tows, steel/steal, stair/stare, rose/rows.

Math Activity 14.1: Rain Gauge

Instruction

Explain the properties and purpose of a rain gauge. Students will create diagrams of this common weather tool and mark increment numbers on their rain gauge. Instruct students to draw a long, thin letter U on their paper, so the sides are close together. This is the rain gauge. They will draw 10 short lines on the inside of the U. The lines should be approximately the same distance apart. (If students' skills allow, have them use rulers to measure the distance between lines.). At the bottom they will write the number 0. They will continue going up the gauge in increments of 10.

Difficulty Level: Beginner

Objective: Count to 100 by 10s

Supplies: Paper and pencils, rain gauge, rulers

Extension: For advanced students, explain the concept of milliliter vs. ounces in measurement.

Chapter 15

Rocks and the Weather

Chapter Inquiry Question: What causes rocks to change?

Chapter Vocabulary/Word Wall: erosion, weathering

Inquire: Introductory Activity

Difficulty Level: Advanced

Objective: Demonstrate how rocks can change due to weathering and erosion

Supplies: Water, tray of soil and rocks mounded to resemble a mountain, tray of assorted rocks, magnifying glasses, copies of the activity sheet "World of Rocks" (Appendix D, page 198)

Introductory Activity 15.1: World of Rocks

Interactive Dialogue

Remember when we talked about different kinds of landforms? What are some of the landforms that can be found on Earth? (Responses will vary but may include mountains, valleys, canyons, deserts, etc.) *We also studied the water cycle—how the sun warms the water, how clouds are then formed, and how rain and snow bring the water back down to Earth.*

Changes in temperature, such as a change from very hot to very cold, can cause cracks in rocks. Then along comes rain, pushing dirt and smaller rocks into the cracks. What do you think might happen to the rocks when that happens? (The rocks break apart.)

Sometimes rain gets into a crack and freezes there. Ice takes up more space than water, so it can push rocks apart and break big rocks into little rocks. When rocks are broken down by natural processes without being carried to a new place, it is called ***weathering****. With weathering, the rocks do not move.*

There is another natural process that also helps break down rocks, like this mountain (the rocks and soil in the pan). What do you think would happen if it started raining on this mountain and kept raining and raining, year after year? (Responses will vary.) *Let's demonstrate what happens. As I sprinkle the rain over the mountain, what do you see?* (The mountain gets smaller; dirt and rocks tumble down.)

This is a natural process called ***erosion****. Erosion carries objects like rocks and soil away, moving them from one place to another. A big storm might push water against the shoreline, and then when the water leaves it could pull the rocks out to sea. What do we call that?* (erosion) *Tree roots dig down into the earth and hold onto the soil, but if all the trees in a forest were cut down, their roots would eventually stop holding the soil, and strong gusts of wind could blow the top layer of soil away. What do we call that?* (erosion)

Extension: Encourage students to look for signs of erosion as they travel and take pictures to share with the class.

Instruction

This activity should be used along with the ELA Activity 15.1: Describe It. For this portion of the lesson, students will select and examine one rock closely with the naked eye and then with a magnifying glass. On their "World of Rocks" activity sheet, they will draw a picture of the rock.

Discussion Points

- Where might you find the rock you examined?
- What could have caused a particular rock's shape or color?
- Why are rocks so different from one another?

Inspire★

- Students can rock with the beat of a video titled "Rocks Song" by musician Peter Weatherall. The video is available online.
- To see an animated demonstration of the processes of weathering and erosion, go to the Make Me a Genius website and view "Weathering and Erosion."
- Learn more about rocks with the book *Rocks and Soil* by Charlotte Guillain.

Investigate: Science Activity

Science Activity 15.1: Rock Formation

Instruction

Pile the sugar cubes into a mound inside the pan. Slowly, begin pouring a small stream of water over the sugar cubes. Have students watch as small pits and caves begin forming. Also call their attention to movement as the cubes fall and gradually begin to dissolve.

Difficulty Level: Beginner

Objective: Observe how water can change the shape of a solid

Supplies: Sugar cubes (or chalk), water, pan

Discussion Points

- How does the experiment represent the natural process of erosion?
- Does this experiment tell us anything about where sand might come from?

Integrate: ELA and Math Activities

Difficulty Level: Advanced

Objective: Use adjectives to describe a natural object

Supplies: Wide assortment of rocks (or pictures of rocks), copies of the activity sheet "World of Rocks" (Appendix D, page 198)

ELA Activity 15.1: Describe It

Instruction

This activity should be used along with Introductory Activity 15.1: World of Rocks. After students create drawings of their rocks, they will select words from the list below (or use their own words and phrases) that describe their rocks. Remind students that the words used in this activity are called adjectives. Adjectives are words that describe nouns.

Rough	Smooth	Speckled	Colorful	Dull
Flaky	Heavy	Light	Jagged	Shiny
Sparkly	Sharp	Flat	Crumbly	Cold
Round	Oval	Square	Spotted	Striped
Grainy	Sandy	Gray	Black	Brown
Tan	White			

Other descriptions can be as follows:

My rock is the size of a __________.

My rock smells like __________.

My rock feels like __________.

Students continue to make similar observations for two additional rocks.

Difficulty Level: Beginner

Objective: Use rocks to demonstrate subtraction problems

Supplies: Small pebbles

Math Activity 15.1: Math Rocks!

Instruction

Using the following example, model the activity on the board:

Jace collected 5 rocks on his trip to the Smoky Mountains. When he returned home, he gave 2 rocks to his best friend Thomas. How many rocks did Jace have left?

Next, distribute 10 pebbles (or similar small objects) to each pair of students. Pairs will work to develop their own math-problem narratives.

Using the model as a pattern, encourage students to create problems that include local landforms, students' names, and other familiar information.

Chapter 16

The Layers of the Earth

Chapter Inquiry Question: What does the Earth look like below its surface?

Chapter Vocabulary/Word Wall: core, crust, mantle

Inquire: Introductory Activity

Introductory Activity 16.1: If the Earth Were an Apple

Difficulty Level: Beginner

Objective: Compare the layers of the Earth with an apple

Supplies: Globe, whole apple, apple divided in half, picture of a volcano, object made of iron

Interactive Dialogue

If you hike through a park, over a mountain, or across a playground, what lies beneath your feet? (Responses will vary but may include grass, dirt, stones, etc.)

What do you think you would find if you took a shovel and dug a big hole? (dirt)

What would you find if you keep digging deeper and deeper? (Responses will vary.)

If we could dig all the way to the middle of the Earth, what do you think it would look like? (Responses will vary.)

Actually, no one has ever been able to do that. It's far too deep. One of the deepest holes ever dug was in the country of Russia. It was 7.5 miles or 12 kilometers deep. To go all the way to the middle of the Earth, however, you would have to dig a hole that is 4,000 miles, or 6,000, kilometers deep!

But we do not have to dig deep to know what the inside of the Earth looks like. Thanks to scientists and their special tools, we know a lot about what is down there. We're going to use this apple to demonstrate.

First, there is the ***crust****, or Earth's outer layer, represented by the skin of our apple. The crust is the surface of Earth. If you were to plunge all the way to the bottom of the ocean, you would still find yourself standing on*

the Earth's crust. Even though the crust is so thick we cannot dig through it, the crust is very thin compared with the rest of the Earth, as the skin of this apple is thin compared with the whole apple.

*Below the crust is Earth's second layer, the **mantle**. It is much thicker than the crust, like the white part of this apple. The mantle is so hot that the rocks all melt together. It's like an ocean made of liquid rock. But the heat doesn't stop there! Way below the mantle is the **core**, just like the core of this apple. The core is the middle of the Earth. At Earth's core, it is as hot as the sun. The pressure is so great that it forms a heavy ball of iron and other metals.*

Discussion Points

- Why is the Earth hotter at the core than on the surface of the Earth?
- If iron is at the center of the Earth, does the Earth work like giant a magnet? How do we know?

Inspire★

- The video "Why Earth Science" provides an overview of the study of the Earth by geoscientists. The video helps connect the dots in the entire study of the planet Earth and is available online.
- Specific work of early scientists in developing current models of Earth can be explored using the video "The Core of the Earth," available on the Science Discovery website.
- Share a journey with students in the book *The Hottest Places on Earth* by Jennifer M. Besel.

Investigate: Science Activities

Science Activity 16.1: Earth Model

Difficulty Level: Beginner

Objective: Create a scale model of the Earth's layers

Supplies: Flexible play dough in red, orange, blue, and green; fishing line; copies of the activity sheet "Layers of the Earth" (Appendix D, page 199)

Instruction

After a review of the Earth's layers, students will create a scale model using the play dough. They will first create the small, dense core using red clay to symbolize the hot center. Over the core they will wrap a thick layer of orange to represent the mantle. To represent the Earth's crust, they will use a thin layer of blue and green (blue for the oceans and green for the landforms). Using the globe as a model, they will need to use more blue than green (70% of the Earth's surface is water).

After all the models are complete, students will use the fishing line to cut straight through their model, allowing them to observe the layers. Following this investigation, they will label a diagram of Earth's layers on the activity sheet and add the activity sheet to their Science Notebooks.

Science Activity 16.2: The Density of Earth's Layers

Instruction

Explain that when something is small but very heavy, it is considered very dense. The beach ball, for instance, is larger than the golf ball, but it is filled with air, so it weighs less than the golf ball. The golf ball has more density than the beach ball. What is inside the golf ball is very tightly packed together (very dense), making it heavier than the beach ball.

Begin the experiment by showing students the three liquids: water, vegetable oil, and syrup. Have them predict which one has the most density and which has the least density. Very slowly, pour the liquids one at a time into the glass cylinder, beginning with the water, then the oil, and then the syrup. The syrup will settle at the bottom, the water will settle in the middle, and the oil will settle on top. Each liquid will make a separate layer.

Difficulty Level: Advanced

Objective: Demonstrate the concept of density and its relevance to the layers of the Earth

Supplies: Golf ball and a beach ball (or Ping-Pong ball); tall, glass cylinder (or empty 2-liter bottle); water; vegetable oil; syrup or molasses

Discussion Points

- Why didn't the liquids mix together and spread evenly throughout the container?
- Why did the liquids settle in the order observed?
- How does this investigation model the layers of the Earth?

Integrate: ELA and Math Activities

ELA Activity 16.1: Getting to the Core

Instruction

For this activity, students will write the word *core* in the middle of their paper. From that point, they will change one letter in the word *core* to form another word. Next, they will change one letter in the new word to form a different word and so on, wrapping words around and around the core, each time swapping one letter to create a new word.

For example, from *core* students can create *tore*. From there they might write *torn*. From there they might write *worn*, and so on. (Or, starting with *core*, they might write *cord*, *word*, *worn*, etc.)

Students will have fun seeing how far they can extend their word circle. At the same time, they will have time to explore a dictionary as they search for words to add. As a variation, they can use colored pencils for each new word, providing the activity with an interesting visual image.

Difficulty Level: Advanced

Objective: Create different words from the single word *core*

Supplies: Pencils and paper, dictionaries

Difficulty Level:
Beginner

Objective: Use a measurement device to determine temperature

Supplies: Thermometers; 4 containers of water that range in temperature from hot to cold; pencils and paper; colored pencils (blue, yellow, orange, red); copies of the activity sheet "Thermometer Graph" (Appendix D, page 200)

Math Activity 16.1: It's Hot!

Instruction

Fill containers with water of various temperatures. A cube of ice can be added to one container to create a low temperature.

Label each container with a different letter. Explain that a thermometer measures by degrees. As the temperature of each liquid is taken, students will record the findings on the Thermometer Graph, including the letter of the container being measured. Explain how a number is written when writing temperature (e.g., A = 72°).

When students have finished recording the temperatures, they will place their findings on the thermometer graph, with the numbers in sequential order from lowest to highest. Once the data has been recorded, they can then color the thermometer. Blue (a cool color) can be used at the bottom, and the other colors will be used to show the changes in the temperature, going from blue to yellow to orange to red.

Red—hottest
Orange
Yellow
Blue—coolest

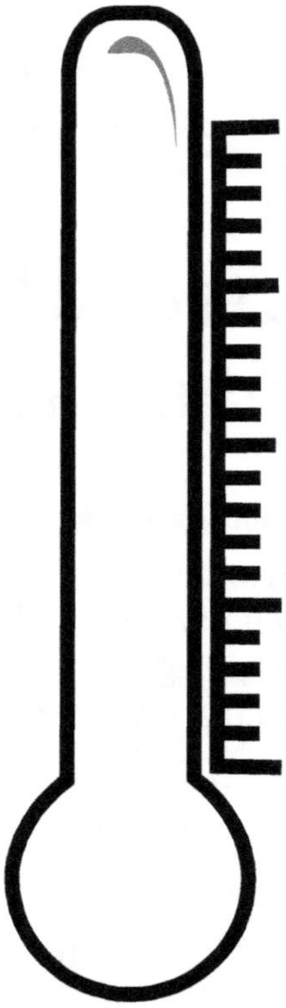

Chapter 17

Earthquakes and Volcanoes

Chapter Inquiry Question: What causes a natural event such as an earthquake or volcano eruption?

Chapter Vocabulary/Word Wall: earthquake, eruption, lava, magma, plates, shifting, volcano

Inquire: Introductory Activity

Introductory Activity 17.1: Shaky Ground

Difficulty Level: Beginner

Objectives: Model the shifting of Earth's plates to simulate an earthquake; model the wave action of Earth's surface during an earthquake

Supplies: Green, yellow, and orange play dough to represent the surface of the Earth; flat pan; water; small rock

Interactive Dialogue

We know that the Earth is composed of different layers. What are those layers? (core, mantle, crust) *We also know that it is very, very hot below the Earth's crust. There's another important fact that we have learned in this unit as well: Landforms can change. What can cause a change in landforms?* (weathering and erosion)

So just as there is change on the Earth's crust because of natural processes, such as weathering and erosion, change also takes place below the crust where all that hot, liquid rock is churning around. Sometimes all that movement causes large masses of rock to shift and bump against each other. ***Shifting*** *is another word for moving. When large masses of Earth's surface shift, the ground starts shaking and cracks form on the surface of the Earth. Does anyone know what is happening?* (earthquake!) *It's an earthquake! An* ***earthquake*** *happens when Earth's* ***plates****, or big sections of Earth's surface, shift and cause large vibrations.*

Instruction

Divide the model of Earth's layers in half. Push the two sections together. Explain how the sections of the Earth, or plates, are shifting—or moving together—which can cause an earthquake to occur.

Next, model the waves on the Earth's surface that are caused by earthquakes. Fill the pan with water and toss the small rock into the pan. Point out the waves on the surface of the water, and tell students that during an earthquake the earth moves in waves like the water.

Interactive Dialogue

A long time ago, these shifts on the Earth's crust caused landforms to lift high into the sky. Do you know what these are called? (mountains, hills)

These are mountains that rise and fall all over the Earth: One way they are made is through earthquakes. Another way that mountains are made involves the ***magma****, or the hot melted rock inside the earth. When the magma gets really active, it pushes against the Earth's surface looking for an escape. This process can form a* ***volcano****, or a cone of rock and soil pushed high into the air by the pressure from magma. That is another kind of mountain.*

If the pressure of the magma becomes strong enough what can happen? (an eruption) *An* ***eruption*** *can happen; that is when the pressure from magma is so great that it pushes right through Earth's surface. During a volcano eruption, hot liquid rock, or magma gets pushed out of the mouth of the volcano. Once the magma reaches the air and starts to flow down the sides of the volcano, it is called* ***lava****.*

Discussion Points

- Describe something similar to a volcano erupting.
- Can a volcano form below the ocean? How?
- What is pressure? What does pressure have to do with earthquakes and volcanoes?

Inspire★

- On the Kids Discovery website, the "Volcano Explorer" will allow students to build a virtual volcano. Set the power of the volcano and watch it erupt. Spin the globe and stop at any location to see where active volcanoes are located.
- A more advanced virtual experience can be found in the video "Volcano Maker," available on the Channel One website.
- A real-time Earthquake Map can be found in the Earthquake section of the U.S. Geological Survey website.
- A number of informational texts are available that illustrate the power of earthquakes and volcanoes:
  - *Earthquakes* by Renee Gray-Wilburn
  - *Earthquakes* by Mari C. Schuh
  - *Fearsome Forces of Nature* by Anita Ganeri
  - *Anatomy of an Earthquake* by Renee C. Rehman
  - *Volcanoes!* by Renee Gray-Wilburn
  - *Volcanoes* by Xavier W. Niz

- The fiction text *The Secret Warning* by Susan Blackaby provides a lively look at a volcano's eruption from the perspective of a young girl living nearby. (The importance of literacy is also addressed in this exciting story.)

Investigate: Science Activities

Science Activity 17.1: Volcano!

Difficulty Level: Beginner

Objective: Model the eruption of a volcano

Supplies: Vinegar; water; baking soda; food coloring; 6-oz (30-ml) clear, plastic cups; smaller paper cups; aluminum pans/trays; plastic spoons; newspapers

Instruction

Provide work areas and cover each with newspaper. Distribute the cups and instruct students to place them in the middle of their aluminum pan. Have students fill their small paper cups with half vinegar and half water, but not to overflowing! They can add a drop of food coloring of their choice. They then pour this solution into their clear plastic cup. Next, they get a spoonful of baking soda and add it to the large cup. The excitement explodes as volcanoes erupt!

Science Activity 17.2: It's a Blast!

Difficulty Level: Advanced

Objective: Model the eruption of a volcano

Supplies: Large pan or cardboard box top; flour, salt and water; modeling clay (optional); vinegar; dishwashing liquid; funnel; baking soda; one tissue square; red food coloring; paint; grass and twigs (optional)

Instruction

When it comes to experiments, the class favorite is usually the erupting volcano. Perform this activity as a whole class or in small, messy groups.

In a wide baking sheet or cardboard box top, combine the flour, a small amount of salt, and enough water to form firm dough. Use this to build a volcano around a small plastic soda bottle that has the cap removed and the top clipped off to provide a wider opening.

Build the volcano so that the bottom is wider than the top and allow it to dry for a day or two. Then, the volcano can be painted and decorated (if the students are willing to wait another day before conducting the experiment). Use a funnel to pour about ½ cup (120 ml) of vinegar into the bottle along with a few drops of dishwashing liquid and a drop or two of red food coloring. Place about 1 tablespoons (15 g) of baking soda in the tissue and fold the ends together, twisting them securely. This will give you enough time after you drop it into the bottle to step back to watch the eruption.

Science Activity 17.3: Earthquake!

Difficulty Level: Beginner

Objective: Demonstrate the action of a shift in the crust of the Earth

Supplies: Assortment of different colored beans, rice, oats, and popcorn kernels; tall, clear plastic cup; note cards

Instruction

Pairs of students should select containers and fill them with distinct layers of the dry ingredients. Explain that they are creating a model of the layers in Earth's crust. Once all layers have been completed, they should insert the end of an index card into the crust. The card should go as far toward the bottom as possible. Then, very slowly, students will shift the card slightly up and then down. Have them observe the change in the layers. Compare this to the movement of the Earth's plates and how shifting changes the form/shape of the layers.

Integrate: ELA and Math Activities

Difficulty Level:
Beginner

Objective: Solve 1-digit addition problems and use suffixes to form plurals

Supplies: Pencils and paper

ELA and Math Activity 17.1: Plurals Add Up!

Instruction

Remind students that some words can be changed to represent more than one object by adding "s." Share an example, such as "If we have 1 car and we add 1 car, what do we get?" (2 cars!) Work through the list as a group, or have students copy each problem, placing the mathematical answer on the first line, the word on the second line, and the plural suffix on the final line.

1 earthquake + 1 earthquake = ____ ______________ __

1 mountain + 2 more = ____ ______________ __

1 hill + 9 more = ____ ______________ __

Explain that other words can be changed to represent more than one object by adding "**es**".

1 volcano + 1 volcano = ____ ______________ __ __

1 volcano + 4 more = ____ ______________ __ __

1 natural process + 6 more = ____ ______________ ______________ __ __

Challenge students to think of other words from the unit and create additional addition problems and plural nouns.

Difficulty Level:
Advanced

Objective: Model the process of a volcano eruption using a foldable diagram

Supplies: Colored pencils, construction paper, scissors

ELA Activity 17.2: Foldable Volcano Eruption

Instruction

Support students as they follow your example for creating a foldable volcano.

Give each student one sheet of construction paper. They will turn the paper horizontally and fold it in half (the long way), as shown at right. Next, they will open the paper and fold each short edge toward the center fold, creating a double-door effect. Have them slide a pencil along the folds to make them crisp. Keeping the flaps closed, students will use the scissors to cut small slits down from the top edge, creating a rough top edge to simulate fire and lava rising out of top of their volcano.

Once students have created their foldable, they will open the front flaps and draw the inside of the volcano (on the middle two panels of the foldable). They will then create rivers of hot liquid squeezing between layers of rock. On the left side, they will label the liquid magma. On the right side, they will explain the process of volcanic eruption in their own words. The basic steps of an eruption include the following:

- The Earth's liquid mantle is at its boiling point.
- The magma presses against the layers of rock.

- The pressure builds, and the magma starts moving toward the surface.
- The magma explodes from the top of the volcano.

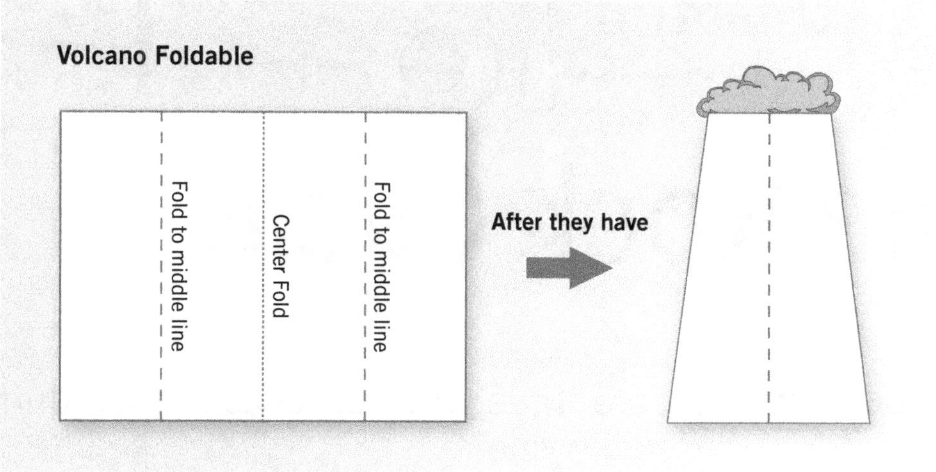

Once they have completed their explanation, they can close the flaps, trim the sides, and create a drawing of the outside of the volcano, using colored pencils and red and orange to show the lava flow. They will enjoy attaching streamers of red, yellow, and orange ribbon to the top. When students complete their foldables, they should add them to their Science Notebooks.

Math Activity 17.1: Get Quaking!

Difficulty Level: Beginner

Objective: Arrange numbers in sequential order

Supplies: Pencils and paper

Instruction

Work together as a whole group to complete this activity. Remind students of the experiment in which a rock tossed into a pan of water created waves. Scientists have developed a Richter Scale that assigns numbers to each earthquake showing the intensity of the vibrations or waves in the Earth's surface. Using the Earthquake data below, work together to list the earthquakes by intensity, starting with the strongest.

Earthquake Data

Year	Location	Richter Scale Measurement
2008	China	8
2011	Japan	9
2010	Haiti	7
2008	Nevada, USA	5
2013	Iran	6

Extension: Students can rearrange the list of earthquake data, this time basing the order of the earthquakes on their dates, from earliest to latest.

Chapter 18

The Rock Cycle

Chapter Inquiry Question: How are three types of rocks formed during the rock cycle?

Chapter Vocabulary/Word Wall: igneous rock, metamorphic rock, sediment, sedimentary rock

Inquire: Introductory Activity

Difficulty Level: Advanced

Objective: Identifying the properties of the three types of rock

Supplies: Small piece of sediment scraped from a rock; examples (or photos) of the three types of rocks (sedimentary, igneous, and metamorphic); assorted rocks for students to sort by type; magnifying glasses

Introductory Activity 18.1: The Rocky Road of the Rock Cycle

Interactive Dialogue

Now that you know more about volcanoes, it's time to keep rocking along. What happens when weathering occurs? (Natural landforms are broken down.) *Weathering breaks down rock into small pieces, which we can model by scraping this rock. The pieces are called* ***sediment****. Erosion then moves sediment, and sediment gathers into a pile where the erosion leaves it. More erosion moves sand and other natural material on top of the sediment. The weight gets heavier and heavier until finally the pressure and heat create* ***sedimentary rock****. A lot of times you can see layers in sedimentary rock. Science is really cooking now!*

*Many years go by. More rocks pile on top of the sedimentary rock until the pressure becomes so great that the rock is pushed deep into the Earth, where it gets very hot. That's when the rock undergoes another change. We now have a third type of rock—****metamorphic rock****. How is Earth like an oven, when metamorphic rocks are created?* (Responses will vary.)

So there's the metamorphic rock, getting hotter and hotter as more rocks are piled on top. It also gets pushed deeper and deeper in the Earth until it gets really hot. It is so hot deep inside the Earth that the metamorphic rock actually melts. In our classroom, it's about 72 degrees, but deep in the Earth's mantle it can be 2000 degrees!

*It can get so hot that finally the pressure is just too much. Boom! What happens? (A volcano erupts!) What did we call all that hot liquid that pours down the sides of a volcano? (lava) Eventually, the lava flow stops; it cools off, and when that happens, it forms solid **igneous rock**. Our rock cycle is ready to start all over again, but it might take a few years—a few million years. This is called a rock cycle.*

Discussion Points

- How is a rock cycle like a water cycle?
- How much time passes from one change to another?
- How could igneous rocks be found thousands of miles away from active volcanoes?

Instruction

Create three stations, one for each type of rock. Include a sample or photograph of the rock type and a list of characteristics. Using the assortment of rocks, provide time for students to examine each specimen and then place it in a station according to their observations.

- Sedimentary rock: tiny pebbles that look like they have cement between them, often showing layers, easily scratched and broken (e.g., sandstone)
- Metamorphic rock: very hard with wavy lines (e.g., marble)
- Igneous: shiny, with crystals that seemed fused together (e.g., granite)

Inspire★

- The Oxford University Museum of Natural History provides an interactive game for students in which they match the shapes as they drag each step of the Rock Cycle into place. It can be found on The Learning Zone page of the organization's website.
- The highly interactive "Rock Cycle" available online at Annenberg Learner provides an excellent opportunity for a whole-class demonstration of the rock cycle through instructive animation. Following the introduction, a series of clicks will take students on a journey through the following features: Types of Rocks, the Rock Cycle Diagram, and finally Test Your Skills.
- Illustrations of Earth's rocks can be found in the book *Rock* by Mary Firestone

Extension: Encourage students to search for different types of rocks on their next hike, identify them, and bring them in to share with the class.

Investigate: Science Activity

Difficulty Level: Beginner

Objective: Demonstrate the properties and model the formation of each type of rock in the rock cycle

Supplies: Crayons, grater with large holes, squares of aluminum foil, two small containers for each student, craft sticks or stirrers, pans/pitchers of very hot water

Science Activity 18.1: The Changing State of Rocks

Instruction

Step 1: With safety in mind, students will gently scrape the side of a crayon against the grater so that the bits land in the aluminum foil square. Explain that the crayon bits will represent sediment particles. They should exchange some of their "sediment" with lab partners to get a mix of colors.

Step 2: Next, they will seal the edges of the foil and press down on their sediment. When they open their foil again, they will have their first rock: sedimentary rock.

Step 3: The teacher or an adult helper will pour hot water into one of the cups. Students will then place their open piece of foil (with the sedimentary rock still in place) on top of the water and observe the softening of the sedimentary rock so that a slight change is observed. They can use the stick or stirrer to nudge it slightly. The pressure and heat have created a metamorphic rock.

Step 4: An adult will pull the students' squares from the cup so that students can observe the changes in the rock closely. They might want to compare their model with an actual metamorphic rock.

Step 5: Pour out the cooled water and refill the cup with very hot water. Place each student's foil (holding their rock) back on top of the water. Now, they should wait even longer, allowing the heat to melt the rock, just as heat below the Earth's surface would melt real rock. As the colors run together, explain that the rock has now turned into magma due to the intense heat. Remove the foil and allow the magma to cool completely. The result will be an igneous rock.

Explain that if students were to shave particles from the rock, the cycle would begin all over again: This is the rock cycle!

Integrate: ELA and Math Activities

Difficulty Level: Beginner

Objective: Create an imaginative narrative about the rock cycle

Supplies: Pencils, colored markers

ELA Activity 18.1: Rock Star

Instruction

Students will complete a first-person narrative about their life as a rock. Read the story prompts below to help students move through the rock cycle. Examples of student responses follow each prompt in parentheses.

1. I loved my life living with my rock family. One day, however, a huge rock fell on top of us. Then I . . . (broke into small pieces).

2. Now I am with a bunch of other sediment pals. We are just getting to know each other. Oh no! Look! It's a terrible thunderstorm. We're moving together in a stream of water! Hey! We're all . . . (crashing together on top of each other, becoming one rock).
3. Hey! Who turned out the lights? We're all smashed together. Get off my head! We must be . . . (pushed together below ground).
4. Cough! It's getting warm down here in the ground. I feel myself changing. Are more rocks piling on top of us? I can't stand the pressure! I feel so strange. I feel another change coming. (I'm turning into a metamorphic rock).
5. I'm feeling a bit wavy and dizzy today. I didn't think I could get any hotter, but wait! Something is happening! I can't feel my feet, my legs. I'm . . . (melting into hot lava).
6. Hey, guys? Do you hear a rumble? Is that someone's stomach? What's that noise? I think I need some airrrrrr! Where did everybody go? (I think a volcano is erupting.)
7. Home at last! Now I know more about . . . (the rock cycle).

Math Activity 18.1: Rock Swap

Difficulty Level: Beginner

Objective: Select numbers to use for addition problems

Supplies: Small rocks, markers, pencils and paper, paper bags

Instruction

Step 1: One student in each pair obtains 10 rocks, a marker, and a paper bag.

Step 2: With the marker, the students write a number (1–10 or higher, depending on student ability levels) on one side of each rock and then place the rocks into the bag.

Step 3: Each student pulls one rock from the bag. Pairs place their rocks beside each other with the numbers facing up.

Step 4: On individual sheets of paper, the two students add the two numbers.

Step 5: When a certain period of time (e.g., 30 seconds) has passed, the two students in each pair swap papers to compare answers. If the numbers are different, they start all over again.

Step 6: Once students both have the same number, they fold their sheet of paper down over the first math problem, place the rocks back into the bag, and begin again.

Step 7: The activity continues in the same manner until students have folded their paper all the way to the bottom of the page.

Variations

- Use three or more rocks for each addition problem.
- Change the activity to subtraction or multiplication.
- Have a mental battle without use of paper.
- Have each student predict if the rock pulled will be an even or odd number.

Chapter 19

Soil

Chapter Inquiry Question: What is soil, and why does soil differ from one place to another?

Chapter Vocabulary/Word Wall: decompose, organism, soil

Inquire: Introductory Activity

Difficulty Level: Beginner

Objective: Describe different soil samples

Supplies: Soil samples, magnifying glass, strainers, water, measuring containers, small buckets, hand wipes, several copies per student of the activity sheet "Soil Samples" (Appendix D, page 201)

Introductory Activity 19.1: When Soil Breaks Down

Interactive Dialogue

*Not all natural pieces moved by erosion turn into rock. Some tiny objects—like fallen leaves, dead flower blooms, even dead bugs—gradually decompose and blend together. The word **decompose** means "break down into simpler substances." Name another word we have studied that we use to describe the breakdown of natural objects.* (weathering)

Decomposed natural material is full of all the important substances that plants need to grow, like tiny living material. That's why many gardeners and farmers add decomposed materials to their gardens; it helps their plants grow.

Some materials—like apple cores, eggshells, or even dead worms—take a very short time to decompose. That's because these are natural objects; man-made objects like steel and plastic take much longer to decompose.

*Decomposed, natural materials combine and are mixed together with water and air. This whole mixture is called **soil**. Although you can't see them with your eye, thousands of microscopic **organisms**, or living things, are in one tiny cup of soil.*

What would happen if we didn't have good, rich soil? (Responses will vary but may include: We couldn't grow plants. Animals wouldn't have anything to eat. Trees couldn't grow.)

Instruction

Provide soil samples from different areas, each labeled with a letter. (Also have students bring a small bag of dirt from their own backyards.) Provide magnifying glasses so that students can see tiny objects in the sample. Have plenty of wipes available, because this is a dirty activity!

Distribute copies of the "Soil Samples" activity sheet. (Students will complete one activity sheet for each soil sample they examine.) Provide time for students to explore each sample and complete an activity sheet.

Have students follow these steps to measure the amount of water the samples will hold: Measure the water. Place the soil sample in the strainer. Add the measured amount of water. Measure the water that goes through the soil and out of the strainer. Record data. (Support students as needed.)

Remind students to label each chart with a letter (in the space indicated on the activity sheet) to match the soil's label.

After students complete a chart for each sample, they can staple their charts together and add them to their Science Notebooks.

Discussion Points

- How important is soil in our lives?
- Why is soil different from one place to the next?
- What is the difference between rich soil and poor soil?

Extension: Encourage students to discover the fruits that grow best in their area. Grapes, for example, grow best in soil that is well drained. "Pick your own" farms can be found in most regions.

Inspire★

- The Natural Resources Conservation Service branch of the United States Department of Agriculture has blended science with history in Chapter 1 of "Soil Stories," available on the organization's website.
- Take a virtual tour of organisms underground with "Underground Adventure" on the U.S. Environmental Protection Agency's website.
- Explore soil on the Discovery Education website. Three topics are available: "Down and Dirty," "Field Guide," and "Soil Safari."
- A "Sammy the Soil" coloring book is on the educational resources page of the U.S. Environmental Protection Agency's website.
- More information on soil can be found in the following books:
  - *Soil* by Cassie Mayer
  - *Soil Basics* by Mari Schuh
  - *Soil Basics* by Carol K. Lindeen
  - *Using Soil by* Sharon Katz Cooper
  - *Rocks and Soil* by Charlotte Guillain

Investigate: Science Activities

Difficulty Level: Beginner

Objective: Observe the various materials that make up our soil

Supplies: Soil, empty plastic bottles or clear containers with lids, water, funnels (or pieces of paper to roll into funnels)

Science Activity 19.1: What's in Your Soil?

Instruction

Step 1: Divide the class into teams and distribute containers and soil samples.

Step 2: Students add soil to the container and fill the container with water, then shake it vigorously.

Step 3: Allow time for the soil to settle. (This would be a good time to view one of the "Inspire" resources.)

Step 4: Once the soil has settled, the students will observe the separation of materials.

Step 5: In their Science Notebooks, students will draw their container and label the different layers of material (e.g., floating leaves, sand, tiny rocks).

Difficulty Level: Beginner

Objective: Demonstrate how some mixtures of soil hold water better than others, allowing for better plant growth for some plants

Supplies: Water; stopwatches; measuring devices; quart plastic bags; scissors; buckets of soil; an assortment of natural materials including: sand, grass, small pebbles, clay, leaves, and pine straw; copies of the activity sheet "Soil Mixtures and Plant Growth" (Appendix D, page 202)

Science Activity 19.2: Soil Mixtures and Plant Growth

Instruction

After finishing this activity, students should keep their completed activity sheets; they will need them for ELA Activity 19.1: Plant Growth Interpretation. Explain to students that they will be conducting an experiment to create a soil mixture that will hold the most water for the longest period of time (allowing for good plant growth) and another mixture that cannot hold water (and is therefore not suitable for growing plants).

Step 1: After dividing students into teams, give two quart bags to each team, along with a copy of the activity sheet "Soil Mixtures and Plant Growth."

Step 2: As students create their soil mixtures, they will list each ingredient and the amount used on their activity sheets.

Step 3: Holding one bag of soil over/inside of another bag, students will use scissors to snip a small hole in the bottom of the bag to allow for drainage.

Step 4: With the bag of soil still over/inside the other bag, students will first note the time. Then, they will pour a measured amount of water into the bag. After the water quits flowing, students will mark the end time on their activity sheets.

Step 5: Students repeat the experiment using a second mixture of soil. They should make sure that the hole they cut in the bag is about the same size hole as in the first experiment.

Gather as a group to discuss the results of the experiment, focusing on the differences between the ingredients and absorbency of the two samples. Discuss possible reasons for the differences in draining time (absorbency).

Integrate: ELA and Math Activities

ELA Activity 19.1: Plant Growth Interpretation

Instruction

Referring to the data recorded on their activity sheets, students will write a paragraph explaining how the two samples were alike and how they were different. The paragraphs should begin with a sentence that states their main idea (a thesis statement, which will probably be an explanation of the purpose of the experiment). They will then provide supporting details about how the two samples were alike and how they were different. The last sentence will provide the results of the experiment. (As necessary, use this as a modeling activity, incorporating student descriptions as you create the paragraph.)

Difficulty Level: Beginner

Objective: Write a comparison/contrast paragraph

Supplies: Pencil and paper; students' copies of the completed activity sheets from Science Activity 19.2: Soil Mixtures and Plant Growth.

Math Activity 19.1: Break It Down!

Instruction

Modify this activity depending on your students' ability levels.

Compare the decomposition of soil to the decomposition of numbers, developing the understanding that numbers also can be broken down. Begin by providing some examples as follows:

16 = 1 ten + 6 ones

362 = 3 hundreds + 6 tens + 2 ones

Write the following place-values table on the board or chart paper, providing an assortment of numbers for students to decompose, as shown below. Students can copy the table, or the whole group can work together.

Difficulty Level: Beginner to Advanced

Objective: Decompose numbers in the base-10 number system according to their place value

Supplies: Pencil and paper, set of two- to five-digit numbers

	ten thousands	*thousands*	*hundreds*	*tens*	*ones*
23,563	2	3	4	6	3
467					

Chapter 20

Reduce, Reuse, Recycle

Chapter Inquiry Question: What factors contribute to pollution, and how can individuals help protect the environment?

Chapter Vocabulary/Word Wall: biodegradable, environment, landfills, polluted, recycle, reduce, reuse

Inquire: Introductory Activity

Difficulty Level: Beginner

Objective: Build an understanding about the future implications of trash on the environment

Supplies: Newspaper, empty rolls from paper towels/toilet paper, plastic bottles, paper grocery bags, plastic grocery bags, paper egg cartons, tape, scissors

Introductory Activity 20.1: Reduce: Trash Piles and Pollution

Interactive Dialogue

We've discussed how our Earth is a wonderful place to live. We know that the ***environment*** *on Earth—our surroundings in which all plants and animals live—is suited for life. But what happens when that environment becomes* ***polluted****, or filled with things that are harmful to living creatures?* (Responses will vary.)

What does this newspaper have in common with this plastic bottle? (Responses will vary but may include: Both have words written on them. People use both of them.)

How are the newspaper and the bottle different from each other? (Responses will vary but may include: One is made of paper. The other is made of plastic.)

Most of the paper that we use is made of trees. This includes the paper in our Science Notebooks, construction paper, and this cardboard roll. Can you think of other objects made of paper? (Responses will vary.) *Paper breaks down, or decomposes, quickly when it is exposed to moisture and soil.*

Plastic is very different. It takes much longer to decompose than paper does. It takes about one month for newspaper or paper bags to decompose, and it takes cardboard like this box about two months.

Guess how long it takes for this plastic bag to decompose. (Responses will vary.) *Actually, it takes almost 500 years for some plastic bags to decompose. What about this plastic water bottle?* (Responses will vary.) *It can be broken into small pieces, but for the water bottle to decompose completely, it would take hundreds of years. All those tiny microorganisms that decomposed natural materials in our soil do the same thing for paper. They also quickly break down food waste like eggshells, banana peels, and apple cores. These natural materials are biodegradable.* ***Biodegradable*** *materials can be broken down by living organisms like worms and bugs.*

But those microorganisms can't eat some plastic. That's why our ***landfills****, the place where all our trash goes, keep getting bigger and bigger and bigger. We are throwing out more and more material that can't decompose. How can we solve this problem?* (Responses will vary but may include: Use paper instead of plastic, drink from reusable water bottles instead of disposable ones.)

Extension: The number of seabirds killed each year from choking on plastic continues to rise. Students can make fliers to encourage people to properly dispose of bags, bottles, and bottle caps to help protect the seabirds.

Instruction

On the board, write the following headings: Reduce, Reuse, Recycle. Allow the students enough time to brainstorm items and activities that will fit into each column. For instance, going to the store one time instead of making three separate trips will **reduce**, or cut down on, the amount of gas used. A plastic bottle can be **reused**, or used again, to water a houseplant or to make a block of ice for applying to injuries or cooling food for a picnic. Aluminum foil can be **recycled**, or turned into new items.

Next, provide an assortment of items, such as cardboard rolls from paper products, paper egg cartons, and other assorted items. Students will also need tape and scissors. Tell students that their mission is to find another use for the discarded items.

Inspire★

- "Plastic Oceans: 18/09/2012, Behind the News," which is available online, takes a look at how scientists in Australia are charting the origin of plastic that washes ashore. The video also provides information about how individuals can help to reduce plastic waste.
- Watch the video, "How Plastic Gets Recycled" on the Earth911 website. Additional videos at this site provide information about the recycling of aluminum cans and paper.
- The video "Oceans: Why the Ocean Matters," available on the National Geographic website, provides a breathtaking view of the oceans and a brief discussion of how much life is being lost in the oceans due to pollution.

- A quick overview of air pollution and what individuals can do to help—featuring a child's discussion with his mom—can be found on the PBS kids website.
- Two interactive games can be found on National Geographic Kids' website. "Creek Cleanup" and "Recycle Roundup" will give students the opportunity to virtually clean a park or creek of waste.
- "The Rubbish Challenge," available on the Recycle Zone's website will test students' ability to sort items that can be recycled, reused, or reduced.
- Informational texts providing more information on protecting the environment include the following:
  - *Reduce, Reuse, Recycle* by Alexandra Fix
  - *Time to Recycle* by Rebecca Weber
  - *Let's Recycle* by Anne L. Mackenzie
  - *Polluted Air* by Angela Royston
- Fiction texts thematically related to this chapter include the following:
  - *Taking Back the Tundra* by Bob Temple
  - *Rescuing the Rain Forest* by Bob Temple
  - *Protecting the Prairie* by Bob Temple
  - *Danger in the Desert* by Bob Temple
  - *Captain Cal and the Garbage Planet* by Jan Dallimore

Investigate: Science Activities

Science Activity 20.1: Reuse: Terrarium

Difficulty Level: Beginner

Objective: Reuse a plastic bottle as a small terrarium

Supplies: Two-liter plastic bottles, scissors, small pebbles or gravel, potting soil, water, small plants (or seeds)

Instruction

In this activity, students will turn clean, empty plastic bottles into small gardens, or terrariums. Before beginning the activity, prepare the bottles for students by cutting approximately 6 inches (15 cm) from the bottom of the bottle. Then cut a few slits approximately 1 inch (2.5 cm) deep into the cut side of the top half in order to make it easier for students to put the bottles back together. Students will need both parts of the bottle and the bottle caps.

Students will line the bottom half of their bottles with pebbles or gravel to allow the soil to drain. They can also add a shallow layer of filtering charcoal (not the kind used for outdoor grilling) to keep the water clean.

Next students add the soil, about three to four inches (7.5 to 10 cm). Students will then select plants or seeds. Plants will need to be firmly planted; seeds will need only a light covering of soil. Other objects, such as a decorative rock or a plastic dinosaur, can be added at this time. Students should lightly spray the soil with water and replace the top of the bottle. Students should place their terrariums in indirect light, check them periodically to make sure the soil stays moist, and watch their gardens grow!

Science Activity 20.2: Recycle: Paper

Difficulty Level: Beginner

Objective: Demonstrate the process of recycling

Supplies: Newspapers, spoons, aluminum foil, water, containers, cornstarch, paper towel

Instruction

Making paper using screens and blenders can be a large, messy project. This activity provides a simpler way to demonstrate papermaking using aluminum foil. The following directions are for student use:

Step 1: Shred newspaper and place it in a container of water. Leave the mixture to sit overnight, so it will get nice and mushy.

Step 2: The next day, add a small amount of cornstarch to the mixture and stir it together.

Step 3: Once the material has broken down, get two sheets of aluminum foil, approximately the same size.

Step 4: Use a pencil to poke small holes in one of the pieces of aluminum foil.

Step 5: Place the other sheet of aluminum foil on a stack of newspapers (or towels).

Step 6: Place a handful of paper slush on top of the aluminum foil that does not have holes.

Step 7: Place the piece of foil with holes on top of the slush and press, trying to get as much water out of the slush as possible. (Note: Before pressing, flower petals, small leaves, or twine can be added to the paper for decoration and additional texture.)

Step 8: Remove the foil that has holes in it.

Step 9: In a separate area, where a layer of paper towel has been laid down, flip the aluminum foil over.

Step 10: Carefully peel the foil from your paper.

Step 11: Place another sheet of paper towel on top of your recycled paper.

Step 12: Then put books on top of the paper towel to help press the paper flat.

Step 13: Allow the paper to dry.

Students can list on their paper the advantages of recycling paper, or they can describe the recycling method that they used. Then, they should add the paper they created to their Science Notebooks.

Integrate: ELA and Math Activities

Difficulty Level: Beginner

Objective: Create a puppet skit to teach a lesson about recycling and to explore narrative writing

Supplies: Paper bags; paper rolls; a variety of recycled materials, such as plastic bottles and cloth scraps; markers; scissors; tape

ELA Activity 20.1: Quiet on the Set!

Instruction

For this activity, encourage students to reuse items that will be recycled! Students will work in groups to create a puppet show to share with the rest of the class. The puppet shows will urge people to recycle. (The shows may depict the journey of a plastic bottle to a landfill, caution against littering, encourage the recycling of aluminum cans, etc.) Explain that skits are like plays, and as such, they are narratives—they tell a story.

As they write their skit, remind students that the title comes first and is followed by the list of characters and the setting. A character's name should be written at the left margin followed by a colon. After the colon are the words spoken by that character. They can also include an adverb that tells how the words should be spoken (e.g., sadly, loudly, happily, angrily). After they have written their skits, they will work together to create their puppet characters, using recycled items. As time allows, the class can work together to create backdrops, reusing cardboard boxes. Then it's show time!

Difficulty Level: Beginner

Objective: Use bottle tops to demonstrate the concept of greater than (>) and less than (<)

Supplies: Milk or soda bottle caps, permanent markers, two half-sheets of paper for each student

Math Activity 20.1: Bottle Cap Math

Instruction

Distribute 20 bottle caps to each pair of students. Explain that they are to divide the caps evenly, so that each has 10 caps. Students will use a marker to write a single-digit number (i.e., a number between 0 and 9) on each of the caps. Every round of play will proceed as follows:

Step 1: Each student selects 2 or more caps and arranges them on a sheet of paper.

Step 2: Students have 30 seconds to arrange one number (e.g., 36 or 248) on their own sheet of paper.

Step 3: When time is up, pairs of students slide their sheets together and decide whether the number on the left is greater than (>) or less than (<) the number on the right.

Students play another round.

Difficulty Level: Advanced

Objective: Use bottle caps to visualize the math operation of squaring

Supplies: Bottle tops

Math Activity 20.2: More Bottle Cap Math

Instruction

Have students practice squaring numbers with bottle caps.

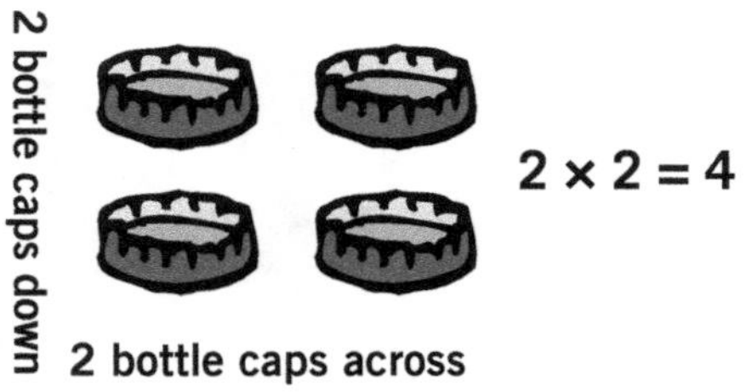

Name: ______________________________

Unit 3 Assessment (b)

1. Circle the letter or letters showing what causes a landform to break down.
   a. erosion
   b. weathering
   c. magnetism
   d. condensation

2. What is an example of precipitation?
   a. rain
   b. evaporation
   c. earthquake
   d. volcano erupting

3. All of these are types of rocks EXCEPT
   a. igneous
   b. metamorphic
   c. seashells
   d. sedimentary

4. Name or draw three things we can do to help our environment.

   ____

   ____

   ____

5. Draw the layers of the Earth and label each one.

©2014 Kaye Hagler from *Inquire, Investigate, Integrate*. This page may be reproduced for classroom use only.

Name: ______________________________

Unit 3 Assessment (a)

Select the letter of the best answer for each problem.

1. Landforms can be changed by all of the following EXCEPT:

a. volcanoes

b. weathering

c. erosion

d. magnetism

2. Condensation turns a gas into __________.

a. another gas

b. a solid

c. a liquid

d. clouds

3. Oops! You dropped your water bottle. The water has poured onto the sidewalk. An hour later, it is gone because of this natural process:

a. precipitation

b. condensation

c. erosion

d. evaporation

4. All of the following are the three main classes of rocks EXCEPT

a. metamorphic

b. sedimentary

c. igneous

d. iron

5. What is the star at the center of our solar system?

a. Earth

b. the sun

c. the moon

d. Jupiter

Digging Deeper:

6. Create a diagram of the three layers of the Earth and label each one.

©2014 Kaye Hagler from *Inquire, Investigate, Integrate*. This page may be reproduced for classroom use only.

7. Name two causes of air pollution. What can people do to help reduce air pollution?____

____

____

____

____

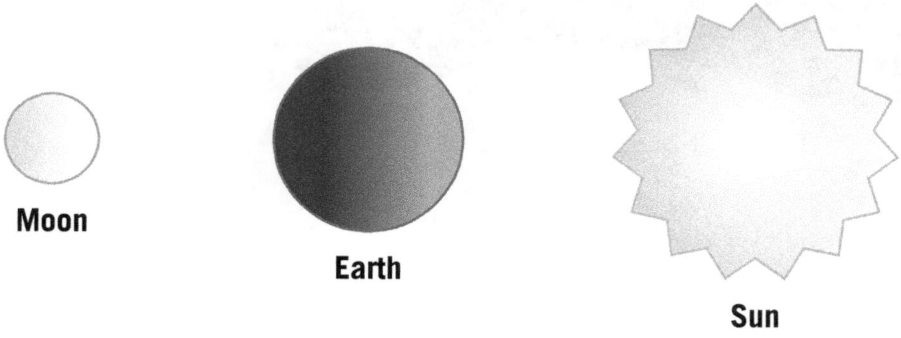

8. Draw arrows showing the rotation patterns of the moon, Earth and sun.

Rotations:

How are the months of the year like a natural process?______________

____

____

9. Explain how we can help the environment by reducing, reusing, and recycling.____

____

____

____

____

©2014 Kaye Hagler from *Inquire, Investigate, Integrate*. This page may be reproduced for classroom use only.

Unit 4

Life Science

Chapter 21

Food Chains

Chapter Inquiry Question: How is energy exchanged in a food chain?

Chapter Vocabulary/Word Wall: carnivores, consumers, food chain, herbivores, omnivores, producers

Inquire: Introductory Activity

Introductory Activity 21.1: What's for Lunch?

Difficulty Level: Beginner

Objective: Demonstrate the flow and source of energy among organisms

Supplies: Interactive whiteboard (or chalkboard, chart paper, etc.), showing drawings of milk and cheese; copies of the activity sheet "Food Chain" (Appendix D, page 203)

Interactive Dialogue

Let's make a graphic organizer on the board listing some of the foods and beverages we had for breakfast and lunch. (Responses will vary.)

OK, so we know that you received energy by consuming, or eating, these items. That means that we are ***consumers****, or organisms, that take in food to receive energy. Consumers can be* ***carnivores*** *(meat eaters),* ***herbivores*** *(plant eaters), or* ***omnivores*** *(plant and animal eaters). Name an animal that is a carnivore. (Responses will vary: tigers, lions, killer whales). Name something that is an herbivore. (Responses will vary: insects, rabbits, cows.) What about omnivores? (Responses will vary: most people, monkeys.)*

Now let's look at the items on the board. We've got cheese and milk. (These items can vary.) *We know cheese is made from milk; where does the milk come from?* (cows, goats) *What do the cows eat to get the energy to make the milk?* (grass, grain, water)

Are cows consumers? (yes) *So, if cows consume grass, where does grass get its food?* (Responses will vary: the sun.)

Actually, grass is an example of a ***producer****, or an organism that makes (or produces) its own food. It receives its energy from the sun, the soil, and water. Grass is at the bottom of what is known as the food chain.*

*A **food chain** is a line of organisms that are linked together by what they eat. So we can put our cow at the top of the food chain, and the grass at the bottom . . . unless . . . Are there any consumers here who eat beefsteaks, ribs, or hamburgers?* (Yes.) *Then who do you suppose will go at the top of that particular food chain?* (people) *People are consumers. So are you a carnivore, an herbivore, or an omnivore? Why?* (Responses will vary.)

Extension: Unlike most plants, Spanish moss doesn't need soil to grow. It feeds off of the air. Many tropical air plants have colorful blooms. Students might enjoy growing an air plant in the classroom or in their home.

Instruction

Using the "Food Chain" activity sheet, note each item that provides energy for plant and animal growth, beginning with the sun. A line of questioning can go like this: "The sun feeds the plants. What eats the plants?" (the grasshopper), and so on, up to the eagle.

Discussion Points

- According to the diagram, what do all of the items represented have in common?
- How is energy exchanged?
- How could this food chain be extended? In other words, what might eat the bird?
- How can a food chain start all over again? What might happen to the food chain if one of the links (like the grasshopper) disappeared?

If you'd like to assess students' understanding, a quick quiz on this particular food chain can be found on the BBC's education website. Type the word *education* into the search box, then search for "food chains."

Investigate: Science Activities

Science Activity 21.1: Fishing for a Food Chain

Difficulty Level: Beginner

Objective: Create a model of a food chain

Supplies: Large and small paper plates, fishing line, hole puncher, construction paper scraps, glue

Instruction

Students will be making a model food chain using fish. While other food chains could be used, younger students might get a bit squeamish thinking about a rabbit or deer being pulled apart by a predator. A fish food chain seems like a happy medium.

Instruct students to cut a large slice of pie from the largest paper plate. Notch the large section of the plate, and attach the smaller piece as the tail. The ruffled edges of paper plates can be added as fins, or students can create their own.

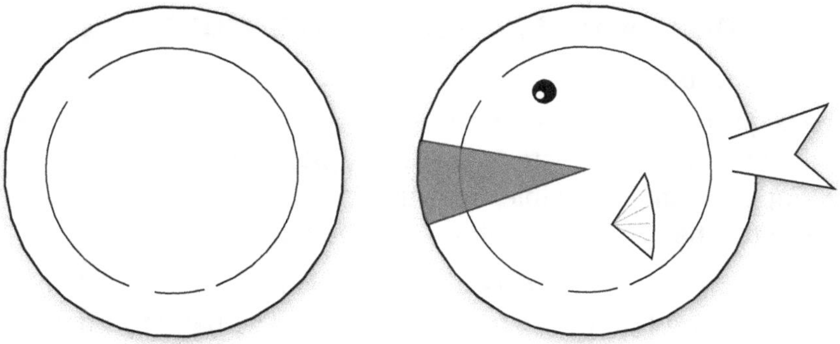

Repeat these instructions using the smaller plate. Students can then use markers and small scraps of construction paper to create the scales.

Many students will want to make more fish to add to the chain. These can be created by drawing around objects, such as cans or bottles, to create circles in a variety of sizes and then cutting those circles from paper plates.

Once the fish are completed, punch a hole in the top and bottom of each one (except the largest fish, which will go on the top of the food chain, and only needs a hole at the bottom). Cut an extra long string of fishing line. Tie one end around the hole in the largest fish, then space the next fish farther down the line, again tying off at the punched hole to keep it secure. More fish can be added in this same manner.

At the very bottom of this food chain, students will cut a small edge of a paper plate and color it green (or use green tissue or construction paper). This is the grass in the ocean, the bottom of the ocean food chain. Depending upon students' skills, have them label the basic parts of their fish.

Inspire★

- The instructional animated video "Food Chain" on the Turtle Diary website, illustrates sample food chains. (Warning: the rabbit gets eaten.) Additionally, it distinguishes among herbivores, omnivores, and carnivores.
- The "Food Chain Game," an outdoor game available on the Primary Resources U.K. website, will keep students on the run while demonstrating the food chain. Printable cards can be laminated and distributed to students. Students will then scurry around trying to find and link with other members of their food chain.
- Students will also enjoy matching the correct order of various food chains as they play "The food chain game" on the Brain Pop website.
- An informational/nonfiction center on food chains can be made using the following books:
  - *Food Chains* by Suzanne Slade and Lisa J. Amstutz
  - *What Eats What in an Ocean Food Chain* by Suzanne Slade
  - *What Eats What in a Forest Food Chain* by Lisa J. Amstutz
  - *What Eats What in a Desert Food Chain* by Suzanne Slade
  - *Staying Alive: The Story of a Food Chain* by Jacqui Bailey
  - *Flesh-Eating Machines: Maggots in the Food Chain* by June Presler

Difficulty Level: Beginner

Objective: Create a food web to demonstrate the interdependence of organisms through the food they eat in the creation of a food web

Supplies: List of organisms (e.g., shrimp, mouse, alligator, bear, grasshopper, rabbit, seagull); ball of yarn; sheet of paper; tape (or pins)

Science Activity 21.2: Who's Hungry?

Instruction

Assign, or allow students to select, an organism. Students will write the name of their organism on a sheet of paper and attach it to their shirts so that the name is visible from the front. Have all students form a circle. The teacher, or leader, will be the "human" organism to start the game.

Holding the end of the yarn, the "human" will begin: "Who's hungry? ***I'm*** hungry, and I'm hungry for __________." The ball of yarn will be tossed to the organism named by the "human."

That organism takes hold of the length of yarn and continues: "Who's hungry? I'm hungry, and I'm hungry for __________." Again the ball of yarn will be tossed.

Continue in this manner until a web is formed. Students should be cautioned to select an organism that would most likely be part of its diet. (A grasshopper should not select a grizzly bear!) While there may be mistakes in diet selections, the focus is on the creation of a web to demonstrate that food chains overlap.

As time allows, students can research their organism to discover its complete dietary habits. They can draw a picture of their organism or find a picture online to copy on a sheet of paper. Then, they can list and draw some of the foods their organism eats.

Integrate: ELA and Math Activities

Objective: Produce a researched-based project

Supplies: Books, library, Internet, paper, pencils

ELA Activity 21.1: Diving Deeper

Instruction

Students will conduct research on their designated organism (from the previous activity) using books or the Internet. They will gather and record the following information:

- What does it look like?
- What does it sound like?
- What does it eat?
- Where does it live?

They will list the information they find in their own words. Then, they will use their research to write a paragraph or essay.

Extension: In place of a traditional essay, have students create a digital essay using photos and researched information. Students can type the information, or, if the technology is available, they can use a voice-over in their presentation.

Math Activity 21.1: Life Span Bar Graph

Instruction

Using the data given on average life spans of organisms, have students represent the data on a bar graph.

Average Life Span
Camel: 40 Years
Cat: 15 Years
Worker Bee: 1 Year
Dog: 20 Years
Goat: 10 Years

(More life span information can be found online at the Texas Parks & Wildlife website.)

After students complete the activity, gather to discuss the results.

Objective: Produce a bar graph showing the life spans of several organisms

Supplies: Paper and pencils, the activity sheet "Life Span Bar Graph" (Appendix D, page 204)

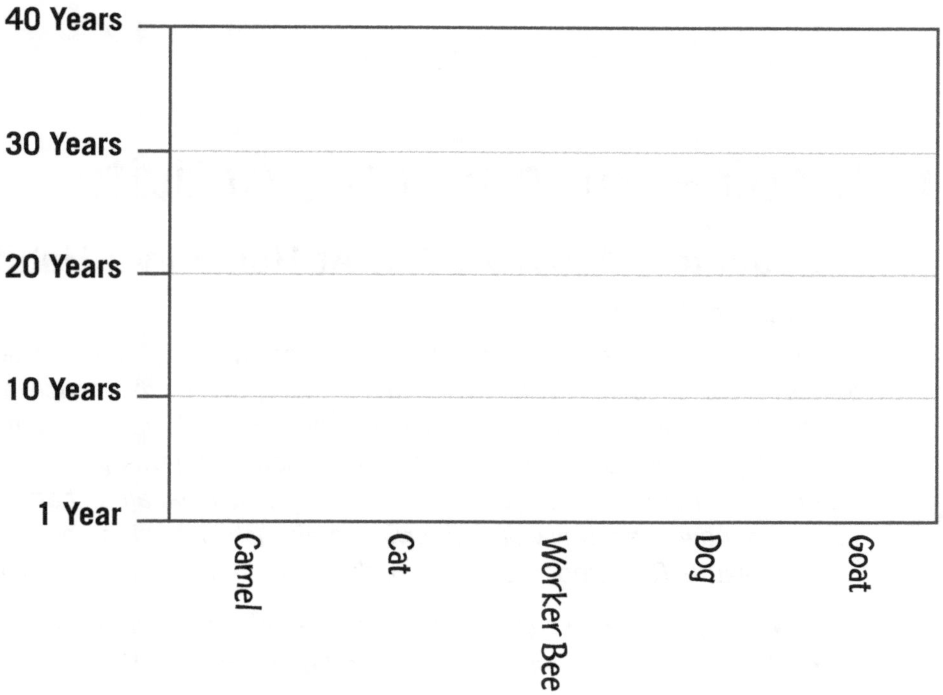

Chapter 22

Habitats and Ecosystems

Chapter Inquiry Question: How are habitats part of an ecosystem?

Chapter Vocabulary/Word Wall: ecosystem, endangered species, habitat

Inquire: Introductory Activity

Difficulty Level: Beginner

Objective: Distinguish between a habitat and an ecosystem

Supplies: Picture of a seagull and a camel, paper plates, construction paper, markers, tissue paper, glue, tape, assorted items for illustrating an ecosystem

Introductory Activity 22.1: At Home in a Habitat

Interactive Dialogue

Observe this picture of a bird. This is a special bird, called a seagull. Seagulls are special because they get to hang out at the beach all day. Have any of you ever seen a seagull at the beach? What happens when people try to have a picnic lunch on the beach? (seagulls gather around) *Seagulls are not particular about their food. They will eat almost anything—leftover sandwiches, tiny worms, berries, crab, fish. What kind of consumer is the seagull? Remember, they eat both plants and animals.* (omnivore).

- *Would you find a seagull at the top of a tall, tall mountain?* (no)
- *Would you find a seagull in the middle of the desert?* (no)
- *Would you find a seagull in the middle of a big city far from the ocean?* (no)

That's because they mainly live close to the beach, which we call their habitat. A ***habitat*** *is a place that supplies everything an organism needs to live—food, water, and a home. Most of their food comes from the sea—unless they can snatch a piece of bread from a picnic basket. When seagulls go to sleep, they crowd together for protection along a beach or maybe in the sand dunes or even on a rocky cliff. When an animal species' habitat shrinks or goes away, the animal might not survive. In situations like that—when a whole species of animals are in danger of dying out forever—we say that it is an* ***endangered species****.*

Now let's talk about the habitat of this camel. Where do you think his habitat might be? (desert) *Camels are well suited for dry areas, such as deserts, because they have very long eyelashes to keep out the sand, and they can store fat for energy in their humps for a long period of time.*

The desert is the camel's habitat, and the desert is a habitat for many other animals as well, along with a variety of plants that can only grow in that area. All these together form a desert's ecosystem. An ***ecosystem*** *isn't just the home of one animal. It's a place where many different plants and animals, the weather, the landforms, and climate work together to sustain life. What can be found in our ecosystem?* (Responses will vary.)

Extension: Even very quiet places, such as marshes, are teeming with life. Students can grab a pail and a magnifying glass, and then head for nearest pond or ditch to observe tiny organisms.

Instruction

In this activity, students will once again investigate an organism. They can keep their organism from the previous chapter or swap for another organism (e.g., gorilla, hippopotamus, elephant, octopus, whale, kangaroo, koala). Using the paper plate as their canvas, they will draw their organism and then complete the ecosystem using the assorted materials provided. Hang their ecosystems all together in a visible location to see the many differences between one ecosystem and the others and to recognize the organisms that share the same ecosystem.

Discussion Points

- How is a habitat different from an ecosystem?
- What might happen if a plant or animal were taken to a different ecosystem to live? Why?

Inspire★

- Webcams provide an opportunity to observe animals in their native habitats. Catch sea otters swimming among redwood roots, a nest of great horned owls, a tropical reef, brown bears catching salmon, plus many more animals in their natural surroundings online at the Explore website.
- Using the online tools "Build an Online Habitat" and "Where Do I Live?" available on the Switcheroo Zoo website, students build habitats for selected animals. Each animal also comes with its own profile page.
- Many informational texts are available to expand students' understanding of habitats and ecosystems:
    - *Horrible Habitats* by Sharon Katz Cooper

- *Habitats around the World* by Craig Hammersmith
- *Habitat Survival* by Melanie Waldron, Claire Llewellyn, and Buffy Silverman
- *Amazing Science: Ecosystems* (a seven-book series) by Laura Purdie Salas

• Literary/fiction texts that support the themes in this chapter include the following:
  - *War Over the Wetlands* by Bob Temple
  - *Treetop Trauma* by Robin Laurie and Chris Laurie
  - *Tide Pool Trouble* by Michelle Lord

Investigate: Science Activity

Science Activity 22.1: Create an Ecosystem

Difficulty Level: Beginner

Objective: Create a model of an ecosystem

Supplies: Plastic two-liter bottles, gravel, soil, sand, bean and grass seeds, snails, worms, moss, assorted insects, dead leaves, strong clear tape, copies of the activity sheet "My Ecosystem" (Appendix D, page 205)

Instruction

Ask students to check their backyards for materials, including bugs, insects, scoops of dirt from under rocks, and so on. Ask that they bring these in plastic bags with tiny holes punched for air circulation. This activity can be performed individually, in pairs, or in teams.

While ecosystems have a few elements in common, students will devise their own ecosystems, selecting and recording the material they use.

First, prepare the bottles for the students. The top three inches (7.62 cm) will need to be cut off and kept for later use. Distribute the bottles. All students will need to put approximately ½ inch (1.25 cm) of gravel in the bottom of the bottles, followed by a good layer of topsoil.

Next, students can choose from a variety of items, adding a layer of sand, or gravel, or dead leaves. The only requirement is that they record all items used in sequential order, along with the approximate amount. Once they have their base, they can add the other materials. Remind them that seeds should only be lightly covered with soil.

Once students have created their ecosystems, they will lightly dampen the soil with water. Then they should turn the top of their bottle upside down and place it on top of their ecosystem. The top will be inside the bottom half. Use the tape to secure the two sections.

Students will use the activity sheet "My Ecosystem" to record each observation, describing any changes taking place from one observation date to the next. They will need to be careful to monitor the soil, keeping it slightly damp until plants are established. Any additions of water or soil should be recorded. When the activity is complete, students should add their activity sheet to their Science Notebooks.

Students can also experiment with placement of the ecosystem, a sunny to moderate environment. If worms are involved, they should place their ecosystem in a darker location or place a paper bag over the bottle to screen and soften the light.

Extension: Introduce the problem of glaciers' melting due to the warming of the atmosphere. Suggest that students investigate their own questions related to global warming. For example: What sources of pollution contribute most to global warming?

Integrate: ELA and Math Activities

ELA Activity 22.1: Save Our Animals

Instruction

Encourage students to use their best arguments in this persuasive writing assignment. Before students begin, explain each of the four topics by providing examples.

- For the topic "Don't feed wild animals," a supporting detail might be that feeding bears will make them come back for more food. As a result, they will lose their ability to hunt, and humans will be in danger.
- For "Plant more trees," a supporting detail could be that not only will this provide more homes for woodland creatures, but it will also help clean the environment.
- For "Preserve animal habitats," a supporting detail could be that some species of animals have become **endangered**, or in danger of disappearing, because there are so few of them left on Earth.

The topics are as follows, but feel free to create more topics with your students:

Preserve animal habitats
Better conditions for zoo animals
Plant more trees
Don't feed wild animals

Difficulty Level: Advanced

Objective: Write a persuasive paragraph/essay

Supplies: Pencils and paper

Math Activity 22.1: Endangered Species

Instruction

Discuss with students the meaning of the term **endangered species** (a special name given to creatures whose existence is in danger). Use the Endangered Species data below to help students determine how many species are endangered outside of the United States. Then, they can see how many species are endangered within the United States. Create other math problems as you see fit, in order to refine students' math skills and their ability to interpret data provided in a table.

Endangered Species

	Reptiles	Fish	Insects
World	79	83	54
U.S.	13	72	50

Source: U.S. Census Bureau, Statistical Abstract of the United States: 2012

Difficulty Level: Advanced

Objective: Conduct subtraction using endangered species

Supplies: Pencils and paper, a copy of the data table provided in the lesson to share with the whole class (on a whiteboard or chart paper)

Chapter 23

The Five Senses

Chapter Inquiry Question: How can the five senses aid organisms in sustaining life?

Chapter Vocabulary/Word Wall: senses

Inquire: Introductory Activity

Difficulty Level: Beginner

Objective: Understand how senses help animals survive dangerous situations

Supplies: Assorted paints, paper plates, markers, paper towels, water

Introductory Activity 23.1: Sensing Danger

Interactive Dialogue

If you hear a smoke alarm beeping, what do you know? (There is smoke and maybe fire.) *The fire detector sensed the smoke. If a burglar tries to break into a business, his or her movements might set off a motion detector. The motion detector can sense the burglar. Our bodies have senses as well. We have five* ***senses****, or ways to learn about our world.*

- *What sense sees dark clouds forming so we know to go inside?* (sight)
- *What sense can hear someone call out "Watch out!"* (hearing)
- *What sense lets us know whether we are eating a bitter chocolate bar or a sweet milk chocolate bar?* (taste)
- *What sense tells us when the stove is hot?* (touch)
- *What sense alerts us to smoke in the air?* (smell)

These are our five ***senses****: sight, hearing, taste, touch, and smell. Our senses supply very important information to our brains, and they can warn us of nearby danger. Animals have many of these senses as well, but their senses are highly specialized to their needs. Animals depend on their senses to help them find food and as a warning device to keep them safe.*

Some organisms, like the owl, can hear sounds from far, far away. Others, like the rattlesnake, have special night vision. Some organisms have sensory organs that allow them to sense warmth given off by another creature's body, even from a far distance. An organism's senses are very important for survival.

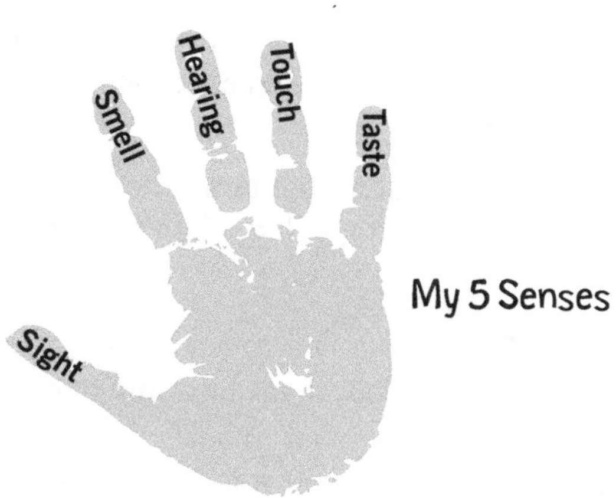

Instruction

In this activity, students will create handprints to help them remember the five senses. To emphasize touch, students will lightly press one hand into a small amount of paint and blot their hand lightly on the paper towel to remove excess paint.

Next, they will press their painted hand into a page in their Science Notebooks. Tell students to make sure their notebook stays open until the handprint dries.

Once the handprint has dried, students can write the label "My 5 Senses" next to the palm using the marker. Next, they will write one of the five senses along each finger. They can add an illustration at the end of each finger with a picture that goes along with the sense written on the finger (ears for hearing, nose for smell, tongue for taste, eyes for sight, and a smaller handprint for touch).

Inspire★

- Students will enjoy "Five Senses Jive," which provides videos of animals using one of their senses, along with a catchy tune. The video is available on the PBS Kids website.
- Dive below the ocean's surface to discover a "Hammerhead Shark's Senses," available on the Animal Discovery website.
- The topic of senses is explored in the video "I Sense," available on the PBS Kids website.
- The literary/fiction text *In One Ear, Out the Other* by Michael Dahl supports this chapter's themes.

Investigate: Science Activities

Science Activity 23.1: Taste Test 1: Sight and Taste

Instruction

Start with either clear soda or lemonade. Mix four different solutions by adding one color of food coloring (orange, yellow, blue, or green) to the chosen liquid. Each solution must be exactly the same except for color.

Difficulty Level: Beginner

Objective: Demonstrate how vision plays a role in taste

Supplies: Small paper cups, clear soda, lemonade, food coloring, pitchers, 4 copies of the activity sheet "Taste Sample 1" per student (Appendix D, page 206)

Pour a small amount of each liquid into separate cups for each student. Have students taste each sample and complete a "Taste Sample I" activity sheet for each sample.

After all results are in, most students will be surprised to learn that each sample was alike except for color. (Don't be surprised to hear "You tricked us!")

Discussion Points

- Why did their senses fool them into thinking there was a difference in taste?
- Why might the appearance of a food or beverage affect the taste?

Difficulty Level: Beginner

Objective: Demonstrate how smell plays a key role in taste

Supplies: Small pieces of apples and pears, blindfolds, small paper plates, plastic forks

Science Activity 23.2: Taste Test 2: Smell and Taste

Instruction

Secrecy is the key in this investigation. Form pairs of students to be lab partners. Place a piece of apple and a piece of pear on paper plates. One member of each team will place a blindfold on the other member. Caution against peeping! Each lab assistant will obtain a fruit plate. While blindfolded, students will hold their noses tightly as they eat each piece of fruit separately. When they have finished, they should answer the following question: Which sample was the apple and which was the pear? Lab partners will confirm.

Next, have students discuss any differences or similarities in taste between the two samples.

Discussion Point

- How did holding your nose affect the taste?

Explain to the students that our enjoyment of food comes not only from what we taste but also from what we see and smell. That's why people with stuffy noses and a cold often say they're not very hungry; they can't smell their food, so they don't enjoy it as much. When you can't smell that apple pie or those French fries, it definitely reduces the flavor.

Difficulty Level: Advanced

Objective: Model the effect of vibrations against the eardrum

Supplies: Rubber bands, uncooked rice or orzo pasta, round containers (cups, empty food cartons), plastic wrap, metal bowl or cookie sheet, metal spoons

Science Activity 23.3: Sound Waves 1: Vibrating Rice

Instruction

Remind students that sounds can be loud or soft and high or low. All sounds, however, are made by vibrations, or waves of sound. Remind them of the earlier experiment with earthquakes using marbles and water. Small waves could be seen moving away from the point of impact. Sound waves work in the same way. They cause vibrations that strike the eardrum, causing it to vibrate. These vibrations become the sounds that we hear.

Students will cut pieces of plastic wrap and lay them across their containers. The plastic must be very tight across the surface. Then they will secure the plastic wrap by putting a rubber band around the rim of the container, making sure the edge of the plastic wrap is "caught" all the way around. The tight plastic wrap is the eardrum.

Sprinkle grains of rice or pasta onto the plastic. Then, using metal spoons, students will hit their metal bowls just above the rice. Stand back as they hit their bowls. The rice will jump from the vibrations created by the bowl.

Many variations of this experiment can be made by substituting different materials, such as parchment paper instead of plastic, marbles or popcorn instead of rice, and other noise-makers instead of the metal bowl.

Science Activity 23.4: Sound Waves 2: Musical Vibes

An additional investigation with sound, and an excellent team project, involves filling similar-sized glass containers with varying amounts of water to create various sounds. Food coloring will add a colorful note to the classroom symphony.

Once the containers have been filled, ask the students to predict whether a container with a lot of water in it will sound higher or lower than a container with less water in it. (A small amount of water has more room to vibrate, thus creating a higher sound. A full glass has less room for vibration, so the vibrations are slower and the tones are lower.)

Next, students will lightly strike each container, creating a sound. Allow students time to experiment with varying amounts of water to create a variety of sounds.

Difficulty Level: Beginner

Objective: Provide varying models of sound production

Supplies: Glass containers, spoons, food coloring

Science Activity 23.5 Match Up 1: Touch

Instruction

Divide students into small groups. Each group should have a bag with several pairs of various objects. Students cannot peek as they reach into the bag and pull out one object. Their task will then be to reach back in and try to find the object's match. Advanced students will enjoy putting a time limit on the action.

Difficulty Level: Beginner

Objective: Discover a matching pair of objects by touch alone

Supplies: Paper bags, pairs of objects in which one member of the pair is slightly larger than the other (e.g., two marbles, two bottle caps, two pebbles, two paper clips, two seashells)

Science Activity 23.6: Match Up 2: Smell

Instruction

Cut a note card in half and attach the identical scent to each half of the card. Liquids can be directly applied to the cards; solids can be taped; powders can be sprinkled onto smears of glue.

Distribute two identical stacks of cards to small groups of students. (Both stacks should contain cards with identical scents.) The task for students will be to match the smells from one stack to the next. This will take a group effort as they sniff to arrive at a consensus on the scents that match. Each stack of cards will then be passed along to the next group.

Difficulty Level: Beginner

Objective: Discover a matching pair of scents

Supplies: Note cards; tape; glue; fragrant/smelly objects, such as herbs and spices (e.g., peppermint, vanilla, lemon, vinegars, cloves, whole peppercorns, tarragon, chili pepper, dried flower petals)

Integrate: ELA and Math Activities

Difficulty Level: Beginner

Objective: Use imagery and figurative language to describe sounds

Supplies: SeaWorld's Animal Sound Library on its website, pencils, paper

ELA Activity 23.1: Sounds Like

Instruction

Discuss with students what the words *cluck*, *squawk*, and *moo* have in common. (They are sounds made by animals.) While the literary device known as "onomatopoeia" may seem too complex at this age, students (particularly comic book fans) will quickly grasp the concept of "words from sounds." Using the Animal Sound Library, students will number the sounds as they hear each one. Next, they will write a word that best mimics the sound. It might be an actual word or an imaginary one: A lion might say "roar" or "urarr." Beneath the word, students will create a simile. (e.g., "The lion sounds like a motorcycle starting.)

Example:

> Baaaa
> The sheep sounds like my baby sister's burp.

Difficulty Level: Beginner

Objective: Create a thunder chart using increments of five

Supplies: Pencils and paper, copies of the activity sheet "Thunderstorm Chart" (Appendix D, page 207)

Math Activity 23.1: Thunderstorm

Instruction

Students will count by fives to create a thunderstorm chart. After seeing a bolt of lightning, many people begin counting the seconds before the thunderous boom. Often they believe that sound travels one mile per second, so if they counted 10 seconds, the storm is 10 miles away. Sound actually travels one mile every five seconds (not one mile every second). The storm wasn't 10 miles away; it was only two miles away!

Create lightning by turning off the lights and then turning them on and off again very quickly. Then, support students as they count by fives until they hear your loud vocal "boom," indicating thunder. Ask student, "How far away was the storm?" As time allows, repeat the activity in order to reinforce counting by fives.

Chapter 24

Vertebrates and Invertebrates

Chapter Inquiry Question: How are vertebrates and invertebrates alike and how are they different?

Chapter Vocabulary/Word Wall: amphibians, class, classify, evolved, fish, gills, invertebrate, mammal, reptile, spine, vertebrae, vertebrate

Inquire: Introductory Activity

Introductory Activity 24.1: Classifying Organisms

Difficulty Level: Beginner to Advanced

Objective: Distinguish between organisms with backbones and those without

Supplies: Pictures of vertebrates and invertebrates, paper, note cards, pencils, and colored pencils

Interactive Dialogue

Earlier we learned that we can separate, or ***classify****, organisms into three categories, or* ***classes****, based on what they eat: carnivores, herbivores, and omnivores. It isn't just what an organism eats that makes it different. We also know that organisms live in certain ecosystems and certain habitats.*

You won't find a camel living __________. (Responses will vary.)

You won't find an alligator living __________. (Responses will vary.)

You won't find a frog living __________. (Responses will vary.)

In many ways, organisms can be alike and different. Let's make a list on the board of some ways that animals can be alike and different. For example, we can add food to the list because animals might eat the same food or they might eat different foods. Who can think of another way that two types of animals can be alike or different? (Responses will vary but may include the following: the way they breathe, physical features like beaks/noses, etc.)

There is another, very important way that animals can be alike or different. Place your hand along your back. What do you feel? (a backbone) *Not all organisms have a backbone, or* ***spine****.*

Can you name an organism that doesn't have a backbone? (worms, spiders, grasshoppers)

Why would some organisms not have a backbone? (Responses will vary.)

Now we can classify organisms another way. Animals that have a backbone are ***vertebrates****. Animals that don't have a backbone are* ***invertebrates****. Are we vertebrates or invertebrates?* (vertebrates)

There are five classes, or groups, of vertebrates. The first class is ***mammals;*** *that's what we are. Let's talk about some of the ways we can tell that we are mammals. What's on the top of our heads?* (hair). *That's one way to identify mammals. They have hair. Also, they provide milk for their babies. Can you name some other mammals?* (Responses will vary.)

The second class of vertebrates is ***amphibians****. This group includes frogs and toads. Amphibians live in and around water. Why?* (To keep their bodies from drying out.) *Their skin is very different from ours. It must stay moist, or it will dry out, and they cannot live if their skin dries out.*

Extension: Invite a guest speaker from a local wildlife service or a veterinarian to answer students' questions about how they help animals.

The third class of vertebrates is ***reptiles****. Snakes, turtles, alligators, and lizards are all reptiles. Their skin is different from ours because their skin is covered with scales. Why would they need scales?* (For protection and to keep their bodies moist so they don't dry out.)

The fourth class of vertebrates also has scales. This group is ***fish****. Fish have scales, but unlike reptiles, which have skin covered with scales, fish only have scales, no skin. Another difference is that fish use* ***gills*** *to let them get their oxygen from water, while reptiles have lungs just as we do. Breathe in really deeply. Your lungs are doing their job—taking in oxygen from the air so that you can breathe. Gills are like thin bands located along a fish's throat. Water passes through the scales. And what's in water? Oxygen! So fish get their oxygen from the water and not from air as mammals and reptiles do.*

Extension: In their Science Notebooks, students can draw footprints they encounter in the woods or park. Later, they can conduct an investigation of their own to discover the answer to the question "Who made the tracks?"

The fifth group of vertebrates is made up of our winged friends. Who are they? (birds) *They don't have hair or scales. What covers a bird's body?* (feathers)

Vertebrates have different outer coverings; some live in water and some live on land; and some are warm-blooded and some are cold-blooded. But all vertebrates have two very important things in common: First, they all take in the gas oxygen so that they can breathe. What is the other trait that vertebrates share? (They all have a backbone/spine.)

Animals without spines are called invertebrates. There are many more than five classes of invertebrates. Invertebrates are creatures like spiders, jellyfish, snails, worms, and octopuses. What might be some other differences between vertebrates and invertebrates? (Responses will vary but may include the following: Not all invertebrates have a bony skeleton, many invertebrates do not have eyes, etc.)

Invertebrates were the very first organisms on Earth. Over many, many years they have ***evolved,*** *or changed. While many invertebrates have very simple body structures, some have very advanced senses. Some can detect enemies with a type of radar or magnetic field. Some move quickly, zipping along at lightning-fast speeds. Others can spray their enemies with a paralyzing drug.*

So which would you rather be? A vertebrate or an invertebrate?

Instruction

Provide materials for students to create a vertebrate pocket foldable on the five classes of vertebrates. Create a pocket folder by folding the bottom of a piece of paper up so that the pocket created is about 2-inches (5-cm) deep. Staple the two sides of the pocket. Fold the sheet in half vertically. There are now two pockets, one on each side.

Vertebrate Pocket Foldable

Once the students have created their pocket folders, they will use blank note cards (or pieces of paper cut into quarters) to list the class and special characteristics of each group of vertebrates. This information can be provided through direct instruction from the teacher, as in the above Interactive Dialogue, or through students' own investigations of books and online resources. Encourage students to illustrate each card with pictures. They will then write the title "Vertebrates" on the front of the pocket foldable and illustrate their folders.

Following this activity, put students' knowledge to the test by projecting a series of photographs on the interactive whiteboard. The photos should depict various animals. You can find many such images at the photo gallery on National Geographic's website. (Go to the Photography section and click Animals.)

You can also use pictures cut from magazines or download them from the Internet, print them, and then glue them onto cardstock. Whatever the source, these photographs will provide a lively session as students call out the names "vertebrate" or "invertebrate" as each photo is shown. For the vertebrates, students can use their folders as a resource to help them identify the specific class in which each belongs.

Inspire★

- Extra! Extra! Read about the world's smallest frog, the smallest vertebrate on record. It's so tiny it will easily fit on the surface of a dime. An illustrated article about the little creature can be found on the National Geographic website. Search for "World's Smallest Frog Found."
- An excellent free resource, "Classifying Animals," is available on the Brain Pop Junior website. A trip to the zoo provides information and illustrations of vertebrates and invertebrates. The site also provides jokes, activities, games, key vocabulary terms, drawing and writing tools, and quizzes. A chart provided under "Talk About It" lets students enter the names of vertebrates and sort them into the five categories.
- The Royal Institution site provides fun and learning with its interactive matching game "Build a Skeleton." Students can follow the clues and build a whale's skeletal system.
- The BBC's Science and Nature site takes skeleton building up a notch with its interactive game "Skeleton Jigsaws," available on the site's Prehistoric Life page. Fossil pieces are put together to construct each dinosaur's skeleton.
- Students will enjoy exploring the following books as well:
  - *Comparing Creatures* by Rupert Fandangleman
  - *Amazing Science: Animal Classification*, (a five-book series) by Laura Purdie Salas and Suzanne Slade

Investigate: Science Activities

Science Activity 24.1: Vertebrae on a Human Spine

Difficulty Level: Beginner

Objective: Create a model of the spine

Supplies: Pipe cleaners, straws, scissors

Instruction

Before beginning this investigation, ask the students to describe their backbone, or spine. What does it look like? Is it just one long bone or a lot of smaller bones?

Step 1: Distribute one pipe cleaner and one straw to each student. Have them insert the pipe cleaner into the straw. Ask them to imagine that this is their spine. Then, have them slightly bend the pipe cleaner and straw and notice the stiffness.

Step 2: Have students bend forward and curl into a ball. Would their backbone be able to bend so easily if it resembled the model?

Step 3: Following this activity, instruct students to pull the pipe cleaner from the straw. Using the scissors, they will cut the straw into several smaller pieces.

Step 4: Students create a loop in one end of the pipe cleaner (big enough to keep the lengths of straw from falling off). Then students thread the lengths of straw onto the pipe cleaner and add a second loop to the other end of the pipe cleaner.

Step 5: Once the model is complete, instruct the students to bend the "backbone" again. They should be able to detect a noticeable difference in its flexibility.

Following the investigation, ask the following question: Why was the model of the backbone easier to bend in the second investigation? Allow students to answer and then explain that the **spine** is a chain of small bones (or **vertebrae**) that encircles the spinal cord (the pipe cleaner). Because the spine is made up of small bones, the body can bend from side to side and back and forth. Demonstrate a few easy movements to show the flexibility of the spine.

Discussion Points

- Why is it important to exercise our spine?
- What might happen to the spine if we stay slumped over for long periods of time day after day?

Investigate: Science Activities

Science Activity 24.2: An Invertebrate Model: Jellyfish

Instruction

Though this is described as a whole-class activity, it can also be performed as a small-group or partner activity.

Choose plastic that matches the scale of your bottle: If you are using a small bottle, you will need to use small squares of plastic or thin food service gloves. If you are using a 2-liter bottle, use a larger piece of plastic. Let students know that you will be creating a model of an invertebrate, or an animal without a backbone.

Difficulty Level: Beginner

Objective: Create a model of a jellyfish

Supplies: Thin, clear plastic bags (e.g., produce bags); water bottles with smooth sides and labels removed; water; scissors; string (e.g., thread, fishing line, dental floss); permanent marker

Step 1: Fill the bottle ¾-full with water and add a drop of blue food coloring.

Step 2: Saving space for a small head in the middle of the plastic bag, shred the tentacles in different lengths.

Step 3: While one student loosely holds the base of the head, the other will add a small amount of water to the bag. Slip this head of the jellyfish into the bottle. While one student holds the tentacles, the other student will add more water to the head.

Step 4: Tie the "neck" securely with the string or floss. Before releasing the jellyfish into the "ocean," place a small dot near the bottom of the head to represent its mouth, where water comes in *and* waste goes out.

Step 5: Replace the bottle's top and move it gently back and forth to show how the jellyfish floats in the ocean.

Discussion Points

- Why didn't we give our jellyfish any bones?
- What determines the shape of the jellyfish?
- What would happen to a jellyfish if it were to be taken out of water?

Integrate: ELA and Math Activities

Difficulty Level: Advanced

Objective: Write a descriptive paragraph

Supplies: Color pencils, sketch paper, old magazines, scissors, glue (or computer drawing tools)

ELA Activity 24.1: New at the Zoo

Instruction

Students will experience the thrill of discovery in this fusion of art and writing as they create a new vertebrate or invertebrate. Like the world's smallest frog, discussed in the "Inspire" section, another new creature has been discovered! Students may use colored pencils, magazine photographs, or the cool tools in the "Make New Animals" activity on the Switcheroo Zoo website. Once the organism is completed, students will write a descriptive paragraph detailing the newly discovered creature's name, classification, appearance, habitat, and eating habits, and any other creative information.

Extension: Compile all organisms together in a "New Zoo" class book divided into two sections: vertebrates and invertebrates.

Math Activity 24.1: Math Bones

Instruction

Students will use their pencils or crayons to color each group of vertebrae according to the information provided on the activity sheet. Explain that the word *fused* means "blended together." When they get the correct answer, they may draw their own features on the head.

Difficulty Level:
Beginner

Objective: Use the mathematical operation of addition to determine the number of vertebrae in a spinal column.

Supplies: Color pencils or crayons, copies of activity sheet "Spine Chart" (Appendix D, page 208)

Neck:	7 vertebrae
Chest:	12 vertebrae
Lower Back:	5 vertebrae
Sacrum:	5 fused vertebrae
Tailbone:	3 fused vertebrae

Color the Neck vertebrae BLUE.
Color the Chest vertebrae GREEN.
Color the Lower Back vertebrae RED.
Color the Sacrum vertebrae YELLOW.
Color the Tailbone vertebrae BLACK.

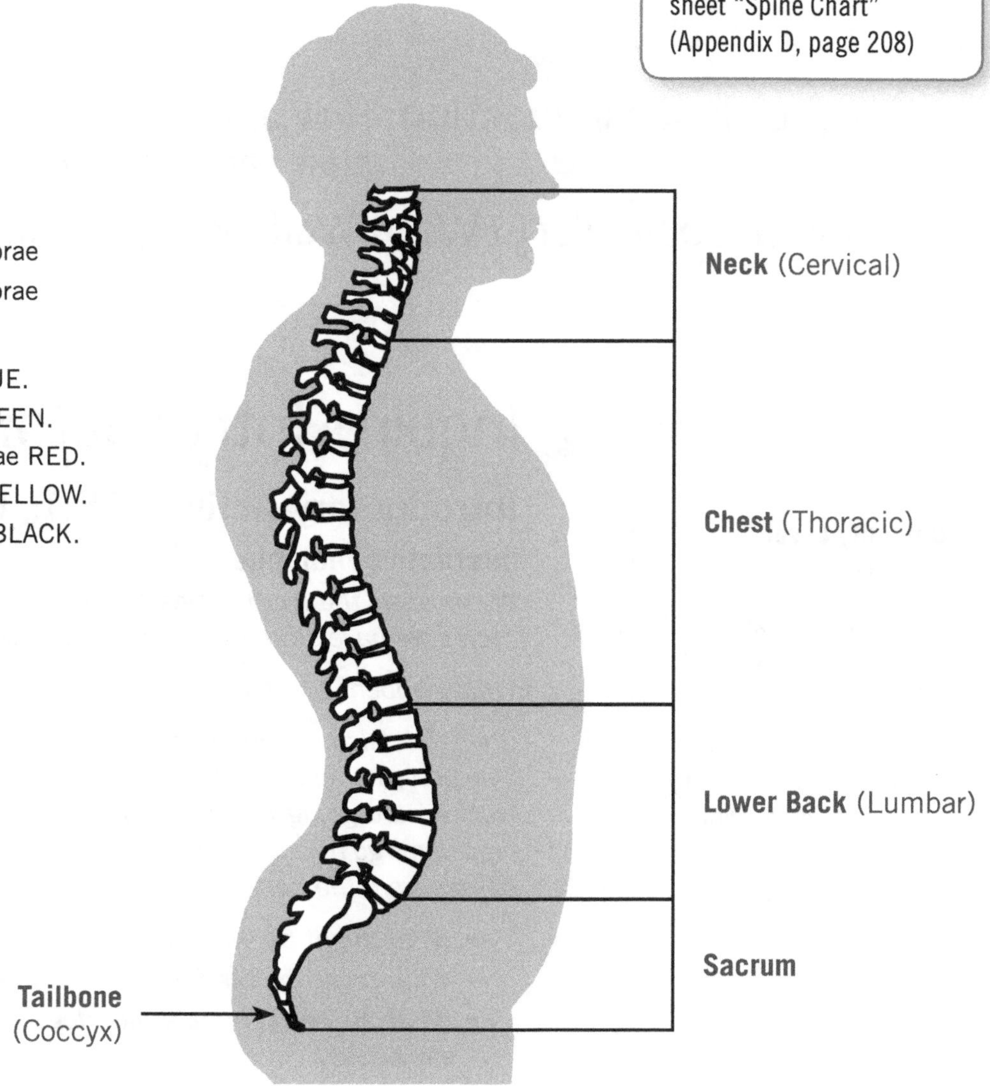

What is the total number of vertebrae? ________

How many more thoracic vertebrae are there than lumbar? ________

Cervical than sacrum? ________

Chapter 25

Life Cycles

Chapter Inquiry Question: How are life cycles of plants and animals alike, and how are they different?

Chapter Vocabulary/Word Wall: life cycle, nutrients, reproduction

Inquire: Introductory Activity

Difficulty Level: Beginner

Objective: Recognize that all organisms go through stages of growth

Supplies: Variety of seed types; copies of the activity sheet "Parts of the Flower" (Appendix D, page 209)

Introductory Activity 25.1: The Stages of Life

Interactive Dialogue

We've used the word cycles *before. Can you remember some of the life cycles we have studied?* (water cycle, rock cycle)

What happened in the cycles we talked about? (Things change.)

Change is also important in a life cycle. Water evaporates and becomes a gas; pressure and heat change rocks of one type into rocks of another type. Now we are going to talk about the life cycle of living organisms. Living organisms go through a ***life cycle*** *also. A life cycle is the stages an organism passes from the beginning of its life until its death.*

- *What might be the first stage in the life cycle of a plant?* (seed)
- *What might be the first stage in the life cycle of a chicken?* (egg)
- *What about mammals like dogs and cats and humans?* (Most will say babies.)

Newborn babies, whether it's a kitten or your little brother or sister, can't do much for themselves when they are real young. But what can they do? (poop, eat, sleep)

- *Who provides their food?* (Responses will vary.)
- *Who changes their diaper?* (Responses will vary.)
- *They are pretty helpless.*

Now, consider a young plant growing in a forest. Does someone come along and give it food or milk? Does someone change its soil? No, but the soil provides minerals and ***nutrients****, the materials needed for the plant to grow. A plant has parts to help keep it in the ground. It receives water from the rain. It uses the sun's energy to produce its own food.*

Plants need the air just as we do. Their leaves are like our lungs or the gills of a fish. They take in air.

Plants ***reproduce*** *by their seeds. When something reproduces, it creates, or produces, another living organism of its own type.*

What would happen if plants, animals, and people did not reproduce? (die out)

Over time, organisms will undergo many changes as they grow and develop. The egg will become a baby chick then a hen or rooster if it gets plenty of food, water, and sunlight. That plant might change from a seed to a seedling then to a twisting vine with beautiful flowers. And what happens to tiny babies? (grow) *They become like you, then me, and maybe even older, like grandparents and great-grandparents. Many babies grow up to have babies of their own. Then those babies have babies. That's what a life cycle is all about—changing and growing until the cycle starts all over again.*

Extension: Students can conduct their own at-home investigations by treating two identical plants differently—varying the soil, light, and water. Encourage them to chart their results and share them with the class.

Instruction

As a class, students will work together to label parts of a plant using the activity sheet "Parts of the Flower." Students can use the diagram as a self-assessment, checking their answers with the responses on the board. Next, students can use colored pencils to color their plant.

After students finish labeling their flowers, gather as a whole group to answer the questions in the section "What's My Job," found at the bottom of the diagram. After completing their diagrams, students can add them to their Science Notebooks.

Discussion Points

- How are life cycles of plants and animals alike?
- How are reproduction and death a part of the life cycle?

Extension: Beachcombers often find welk shells along the shore. But that's not the only evidence of the welk life cycle that washes up onto the beach; the papery thin egg casings also can be observed. Each of these disks may hold up to 20 eggs. Enourage students to keep their eyes open for evidence of a life cycle—seeds, nests, baby birds, or small fragments of a broken eggshells.

Inspire★

- Students and teachers will enjoy a colorful video on the life cycle of a butterfly at the "Animals and Pets" section of National Geographic's Kid's site. Look under the "Bugs" subheading.
- Make the leap from butterflies to frogs by exploring the video "The Life Cycle of a Frog," available on the Turtle Diary website. (Look for the "kid videos" label.) This video uses an animated approach as it moves from the eggs' being laid in the water to the start of a new cycle.
- Quick! Pour on the water—but not too much! The interactive exercise "How Plants Grow" allows students to provide water and heat to keep plants growing. It is available on the Science Kids website.
- Many books are available to further explore life cycles:
  - *Plant Life Cycles* (a six-book series) by Linda Tagliaferro
  - *Animals: Life Cycles*, (a four-book series) by Gail Saunders-Smith
  - *The Cycle of Your Life* by Rebecca Weber

Difficulty Level: Beginner

Objective: Model the four stages of a butterfly's life cycle

Supplies: Several types of pasta, including orzo, shells, spinach rotini, and bowtie; paper plates; markers; glue; small green leaves; green construction paper; pencils; scissors; tiny twigs; markers

Science Activity 25.1: Life Cycle of a Butterfly

Instruction

Give a paper plate and markers to each student, and have them divide the plate into four quarters by drawing a line down the middle of the plate (top to bottom) and a line across the middle (side to side). As you discuss all of the steps in the butterfly's life cycle, have students represent each stage on the plate as follows:

1. The top left quarter should be labeled "Egg." They will trace a leaf on construction paper, cut out the drawing of the leaf, and glue it into this quarter of the plate. Next, they will glue one or two pieces of the orzo pasta onto the leaf to represent eggs.
2. The top right quarter should be labeled "Larva." Explain that this is the caterpillar stage. Students will glue another construction-paper leaf onto this quarter of the plate and then glue onto the leaf the green rotini pasta to represent a caterpillar. The leaves represent the food that the organism eats as it develops.
3. The bottom right section should be labeled "Pupa." Add another green leaf, this time using shell pasta to represent the cocoon.
4. The bottom left quarter of the plate should be labeled "Butterfly," the last stage in the butterfly's life cycle. This time students can tape a small piece of twig onto the quarter of the plate. Colored markers can be used to decorate the bowtie pasta before it is glued beside the twig to represent a butterfly. The butterfly's metamorphosis, or change, is now complete!

Science Activity 25.2: Potato Garden

Instruction

This is a long-range investigation (two to three months), so it may not be suited for every classroom. Begin the activity in January or February, because potatoes like a cool climate.

Individually or in small groups, students will be testing to determine the following:

- Which potato type sprouted better than the others?
- Which potato type grew more vegetation above ground?
- Which potato type yielded the most potatoes?

Each group will record all data over the course of the investigation. Variables include the following (feel free to add to this list):

1. Potato type (sweet, red, Irish, Idaho, organic, etc.)
2. Method of sprouting
   A. Insert four toothpicks into a whole potato and set it into a jar of water so that the bottom stays in the water until it sprouts sufficiently for planting.
   B. Same procedure as above except that the potato is cut in half.
   C. Cut small eyes from a potato and cover lightly with a planting medium.
3. Type of container
   A. A waterproof recycling bag with small holes punched through the bottom
   B. A five-gallon bucket with holes punched in the bottom
   C. Directly into the ground
4. Planting Medium
   A. Potting soil
   B. Potting soil mixed with leaves
   C. Pine straw

Additional pages in the Science Notebook may be used to record data over the course of the investigation. Students can use research skills to identify various types of medium that can be used. The inside stuffing of a diaper, for instance, has been found to retain moisture, and thus could be mixed into the soil. This would also be an excellent opportunity to experiment with the addition of organic materials, such as coffee grounds from the teachers' lounge, vegetable waste, and grass cuttings. Bags will need to be placed in a sunny location that is protected from overwatering if thunderstorms are common in your area.

Difficulty Level: Beginner to Advanced—Independent Study or Classroom Project

Objective: Experiment with several variables—such as potato variety and growing mediums—to discover the variables that provide optimal plant growth

Supplies: Different varieties of potatoes; toothpicks; jars; water; buckets; waterproof, plastic-coated recycling bags; potting soil; other assorted materials; copies of activity sheet "Our Potato Patch" (Appendix D, page 210)

Integrate: ELA and Math Activities

Difficulty Level:
Advanced

Objective: Write a compare/contrast paragraph

Supplies: Two video clips of the song "Circle of Life" from *The Lion King* (one from the movie and the other from the Broadway musical, available online); the song's written lyrics

ELA Activity 25.1: Circles of Life

Instruction

As students view the two clips, encourage them to make notes in a labeled two-column chart or a Venn diagram. A previewing discussion could address how movies and live performances often differ and why songs are often different from one medium to another.

As they view the videos, students should include the following details:

- The song's main (big) idea
- Details that support the main idea and how the details are different and the same from one video to the other.

After screening both video clips, discuss students' observations and preferences as a whole group. Before students start writing, provide copies of the lyrics to support their writing efforts.

Extension: Students could extend their paragraphs into essays to make more in-depth comparisons among characters, settings, and main and minor ideas.

Math Activity 25.1: What's Up at the Zoo?

Difficulty Level: Advanced

Objective: Use addition and subtraction with data

Supplies: pencils and paper

Instruction

This activity can be performed as a whole-class activity. Announce to the students that the local zoo has had an explosion of births! It will be students' job to count the animals and calculate the total number of animals now living in the zoo. Before all of the babies were born, there were 251 animals.

The following animals were recently born:

- 4 lion cubs
- 1 elephant calf
- 9 rattlesnakes
- 25 mice pups
- 5 ducklings

However:

1 old giraffe caught a disease and died
1 duck was eaten by an alligator
3 mice were eaten by a rattlesnake

Use the data to answer the following questions:

- How many animals were added to the zoo?
- How many were taken away?
- What is the population of the zoo now?

Name: ____

Unit 4 Assessment (b)

1. A dog is this type of organism:

a. reptile

b. amphibian

c. mammal

d. fish

2. A cow is an herbivore because it only eats _________.

a. birds

b. plants

c. meat

d. reptiles

3. Which one is an invertebrate?

a. deer

b. human

c. cat

d. jellyfish

4. Describe your habitat.

5. Create a drawing of you eating a pizza. Name three senses that help you enjoy your pizza.

 ©2014 Kaye Hagler from *Inquire, Investigate, Integrate*. This page may be reproduced for classroom use only.

Name: ____

Unit 4 Assessment (a)

Select the letter for the best answer in each problem.

1. Which of the following would be considered a producer?

a. tree

b. monkey

c. snail

d. human

2. Which organisms only eat meat?

a. herbivores

b. omnivores

c. carnivores

d. consumers

3. This sense helps us know when a distant storm is coming.

a. sight

b. sound

c. taste

d. touch

4. What causes sound?

a. senses

b. nutrients

c. sight

d. vibrations

5. This supplies everything an organism needs to survive.

a. senses

b. landform

c. habitat

d. waves

Dig Deeper

6. Are you a consumer or a producer? Explain why.____________________

____

____

____

7. Create a Venn diagram showing how plants and animals are alike and how they are different. Use the back of this page.

©2014 Kaye Hagler from *Inquire, Investigate, Integrate*. This page may be reproduced for classroom use only.

Appendix A

Beyond the Box: Scientific Inquiry and Science Education

The scene is familiar. A Christmas tree stands glittering in the background, with the latest gadgets, toys, coloring books, dolls, and trucks littering the floor. But where are the children on this happy occasion? One is building a fort using the box from his new three-wheeler, while another is giving the cat a ride—in the box from her new doll-stroller. The adults—who saved every extra dollar, who just made the last layaway payment, who valiantly fought the Black Friday crowds, who spent the wee hours of Christmas morning assembling Part D so that it fits Part M—look on in dismay. Despite their efforts, the star attractions are the empty boxes, three-dimensional cardboard rectangles, squares, and cylinders that could have been picked up at a recycling center for free.

Children are drawn to the unknown. They already know the car will roll, the doll can be clothed and rocked, and the electronic device needs its battery charged. But a box! A box can be anything. It's an airplane, a car, a rocket ship, a hole. You can sit in it and rock it from side to side; you can pull it over your head and hide. Now it's a dragon's lair, and now it's a bear's cave. If you have enough boxes, you can make a train, a tunnel, or a maze. What child doesn't love boxes?

The Curiosity Factor

According to researcher Sophie von Stumm (2011), children's natural curiosity, or the need to explore the possibilities, is a trait that should be encouraged from the start. Following an exhaustive study, von Stumm and her colleagues provided evidence that curiosity was an important indicator of future intellectual achievement. For science educators, the message is:

Bring out the boxes and the rocks and the seashells; pull out science trade books, even ones created for adults; distribute the magnifying glasses and measuring devices. Materials that allow students to question—"What if?" "Why?" "How?"—are better than any set of flashcards.

Still, there's no need to throw away the textbooks, the formulas, the diagrams, or the charts. In the educational setting, curiosity needs direction and an objective. The results need to be assessed to determine whether the objective has been met. Otherwise the lesson was just a box on the floor. Maybe a good time was had by all, but what was achieved?

Scientific Inquiry: "I wonder what will happen If I do this?"

Despite inquiry's relatively recent climb to the "Top 40 Chart" in science education, Aristotle developed our method of scientific inquiry thousands of years ago. In 1877, Sir Alexander Grant analyzed Aristotle's method of instruction and noted four key components: ask a question, make observations, conduct a hands-on investigation, and search for the cause of an effect. While no KWL chart was handy in Aristotle's time, he nevertheless placed great importance on prior knowledge in approaching a topic of study. As Grant explains, "He set out all that was known or believed on each subject, and added to the knowledge or criticized the belief as well he could" (144).

Aristotle was right to criticize—just as later scientists were right to criticize him and his theories, many of which they proved inaccurate (see Chapter 7: Mass and Falling Objects). Indeed, inaccuracies often pave the way for learning: Scientists revisit early concepts, make their own observations, gather their own data, and arrive at their own conclusions—which, in turn, may or may not stand up to the scrutiny of the next generation of scientists.

Fast-forward to 1996, when the National Academy of Sciences published its revised National Science Education Standards, shifting the instructional focus from content (*what* should be learned) to inquiry (*how* science should be learned/science-as-process). The new standards also shifted the role of teachers from dispensers of a rigid, just-the-facts curriculum to guides who encouraged students to use—not merely memorize—new information. Under this new paradigm, information was no longer an end in itself; it became the foundation for students' own inquiries as they observed, questioned, investigated, and interpreted the world.

In examining these newly redefined roles, Anderson (2002), cautioned that to be effective, inquiry-based science could not be reserved for only students. He advocated "science as inquiry, learning as inquiry [and] teaching as inquiry." Implementation of these concepts should, he said, "result in greater or better learning." In other words, in order for scientific inquiry to be successful in the classroom, inquiry needed to become the model at every level—and teachers had to be fully trained in its application.

The "Big Idea" of Scientific Inquiry

The scientific community helped define the basic framework for the inquiry-driven science classroom. In 2005, the BSCS Center for Curriculum Development published *Doing Science: The Process of Scientific Inquiry*. Also in 2005, the National Academies of Science published *How Students Learn: Science in the Classroom*. Both publications emphasized the teacher's role in creating an environment where students are given the guidance, tools, and instruction they need as they work to identify problems and search for solutions—in other words, an environment where the concept of scientific inquiry comes to life. The authors claimed that these interactions between the students and the teacher would lead to an environment in which the following are possible:

- Active involvement
- Making observations
- Examining resources
- Asking questions
- Making predictions
- Conducting investigations
- Gathering data
- Using tools of the field of study
- Asking more questions
- Using evidence to explain conclusions
- Communicating results

This list alone should dispel any misconceptions that the scientific inquiry allows students to boldly go wherever they would like. Doors are open for active exploration, but there is, indeed, a method to the madness: Classroom activities have direction, and student understanding continues to be assessed. The difference between the old and new models is easily illustrated by the following examples:

With excitement, Teacher A places a large box on a table and watches as students grab tissue rolls, string, plastic spoons, rulers, tape, drinking straws, construction paper, and paper clips. His instruction: See what you can build from these objects! After the string gets wound around Charlie four or five times and Claire has made paper balls to throw at her friends, the principal happens to stroll by. Uh oh!

With equal excitement, Teacher B places a large box on a table and then shows images on her interactive whiteboard of four types of bridges. She opens a discussion about concerns an engineer might have when planning a bridge in various locations (near the beach with sandy soil, on a mountain with a steep slope, over a wide river with the possibility of erosion). Following this discussion, she pulls from the box bulging paper bags, each containing identical materials in identical amounts. The teacher divides the class into teams and then issues a challenge: Construct a model of a beam bridge that will span 20 centimeters (approximately 8 inches). Each bridge will be tested to determine whether it can hold two or more blocks.

There will be no partial successes: even a small malfunction could indicate a fallen bridge. Bridges holding five or more blocks will be given a special designation.

In Teacher B's classroom—once students have an objective, a goal, and the tools to conduct their investigation—students' excitement builds. Teams put their heads together, and plans take shape. Before each team tests its model, team members predict how many blocks it will hold. Invariably, after the last bridge has been tested, students will be eager to repeat the process—to correct mistakes and miscalculations. Even failure has proven beneficial to the learning. Along with this science and engineering investigation, Teacher B also presents critical mathematical concepts—measurements and shapes.

The Future of the Textbook in the Science Classroom

So where does the textbook fit into this approach? Whether e-book or print, the textbook is transformed into a more meaningful resource for students. As Ulerick (2013) notes, it is the teacher's role to provide "students more meaningful purposes for reading." Throughout the inquiry process—classroom discussions, questioning, and investigations—the textbook is one of many resources that should be critical to the instructional landscape. In an inquiry-based science classroom, whether students are engaged in discussions or investigation, they will indeed discover more meaningful purposes for reading their textbooks.

The Role of Trade Books in the Science Classroom

Along with the classroom textbook, the teacher who incorporates scientific inquiry into the classroom will maintain a bookshelf of trade books in order to foster growing curiosity, answer new questions, and present new investigations. Also, as Rice (2002) points out, textbooks tend to be dated, and they contain a disproportionate amount of text to graphics—a major drawback for young readers. Trade books leap into action as they:

- Narrow information to one topic
- Ease the frustration caused by the presence of unrelated (and overly abundant) text on the page when students wish to investigate only a single topic
- Connect students with familiar vocabulary
- Provide easy-to-follow text features to facilitate the investigation process

In addition, trade books help teachers build text-rich environments in their classrooms at an affordable price compared with the cost of textbooks.

Making the Most of the Day

Every day in classrooms across the country, teachers face personal evaluation, scores that are tied to student performance, standards that must be tied to each lesson, and a push to use more technology in the classroom. For teachers working under such relentless pressures, developing an inquiry-driven classroom can seem a daunting challenge. It was my goal in writing this book to ease the way for teachers to make those seemingly impossible leaps into the unknown. I've tried to pull compact instruction—"big idea" objectives of instruction; the activities themselves; additional resources; Science, ELA, and Math standards; vocabulary/word walls; across-the-curriculum links; technology options; and assessments—all together in one resource. My hope is that this resource will help get you there. Best of luck!

Bibliography

Anderson, Ronald D. (2002). Reforming science teaching: What research says about inquiry. *Journal of Science Teacher Education* 13(1): 1–12.

Grant, Sir Alexander. (1877). *Aristotle*. Philadelphia: Lippincott, Retrieved from Google Books.

National Governors Association Center for Best Practices & Council of Chief State School Officers. (2010). *Common Core State Standards for English language arts and literacy in history/social studies, science, and technical subjects*. Washington, DC: National Governors Association for Best Practices, Council of Chief State School Officers.

National Governors Association Center for Best Practices, Council of Chief State School Officers. (2010). *Common Core State Standards for Mathematics*. Washington, DC: National Governors Association for Best Practices, Council of Chief State School Officers.

National Research Council. (1996). National Science Education Standards. Washington, DC: National Academy Press.

National Research Council. (2005). *How Students Learn: Science in the Classroom*. Washington, DC: The National Academies Press.

National Research Council. (2013). NEXT Generation Science Standards. Washington, DC: The National Academies Press.

Rice, Diana C. (2002). Using trade books in teaching elementary science: Facts and fallacies. *The Reading Teacher* 55(6), 552–565.

Ulerich, Sarah L. (2013). Using textbooks for meaningful learning in science. National Association for Research in Science Teaching. Reston, VA.

Von Stumm, S., Hell, B., & Chamorro-Premuzic, T. (2011). The hungry mind: Intellectual curiosity is the third pillar of academic performance. *Perspectives on Psychological Science, 6*(6), 574–588.

Suggested Further Reading

Casteel, C.P., & Isom, B.A. (1994). Reciprocal processes in science and literacy learning. *The Reading Teacher,* 47, 538–544.

Haury, D. L. (1993). Teaching science through inquiry (Report No. ED 359 048). Columbus, OH: ERIC Clearinghouse for Science, Mathematics, and Environmental Education. Retrieved from ERIC database.

Lynch-Brown, C. & Tomlinson, C.M. (1999). *Essentials of children's literature* (3rd ed.) Boston, MA: Allyn & Bacon.

Klemm, William R. (2007). What good is learning if you don't remember it? *The Journal of Effective Teaching.* 7(1). 61–73.

Maria, K., & Jung, K. (1993). *A comparison of fifth graders' comprehension and retention of scientific information using a science textbook and an informational storybook.* Paper presented at the 43rd Annual Meeting of the National Reading Conference, Charleston, SC. (ERIC Document Reproduction Service No. ED 364 864)

Moss, B. (1991). Children's nonfiction trade books: A complement to content area texts. *The Reading Teacher,* 45, 26–32.

Ross, E.P. (1994). Using children's literature across the curriculum. In *Fastback 374.* Bloomington, IN: Phi Delta Kappa Educational Foundation. (ERIC Document Reproduction Service No. ED 374–467)

Tyson, H., & Woodward. A. (1989). Why aren't students learning very much from textbooks? *Educational Leadership,* 47(3), 14–17.

Appendix B

Standards Correlations by Lesson

All Chapters

The following ELA Common Core State Standards correlate with the content of every chapter in the text.

SL.K-2.1 Participate in collaborative conversations with diverse partners about *topics and texts* with peers and adults in small and larger groups.

RI.K-1.1 With prompting and support, ask and answer questions about key details in a text.

RI.2.1 Ask and answer such questions as *who, what, where, when, why,* and *how* to demonstrate understanding of key details in a text.

SL.K.2 Confirm understanding of a text read aloud or information presented orally or through other media by asking and answering questions about key details and requesting clarification if something is not understood.

SL.1.2 Ask and answer questions about key details in a text read aloud or information presented orally or through other media.

SL.2.2 Recount or describe key ideas or details from a text read aloud or information presented orally or through other media.

Unit One: Discovering the World of Science

Chapter 1: What in the World?

Introductory Activity 1.1: Our World

2-ESS2.B Maps show where things are located. One can map the shapes and kinds of land and water in an area.

Introductory Activity 1.2: Hot Air Balloon Ride

2-LS4.D There are many different kinds of living things in any area, and they exist in different places on land and water.

Science Activity 1.1: Colors of the World

2-ESS2-2 Develop a model to represent the shapes and kinds of land and bodies of water in an area.

Science Activity 1.2: Earth Toss

ESS2.C The roles of water in Earth's surface

Science Activity 1.3: Landforms

ESS2.B Plate Tectonics and Large-Scale System Interactions: Maps show where things are located. One can map the shapes and kinds of land and water in any area.

Science and Engineering Practices: Obtaining, Evaluating, and Communicating Information Obtaining, evaluating, and communicating information in K-2 builds on prior experiences and uses observations and texts to communicate new information. Obtain information using various texts, text features (e.g., headings, tables of contents, glossaries, electronic menus, icons), and other media that will be useful in answering a scientific question.

ELA Activity 1.1: A New Kid in Town

SL.K.4 Describe familiar people, places, things, and events and, with prompting and support, provide additional detail.

ELA Activity 1.2: Letter from Earth

SL.1.4 Describe people, places, things, and events with relevant details, expressing ideas and feelings clearly.

ELA Activity 1.3: Glorf Compared with Earth

W.1.2 Write informative/explanatory texts in which they name a topic, supply some facts about the topic, and provide some sense of closure.

Activity 1.4: Save Planet Earth!

W.2.1 Write opinion pieces in which they introduce the topic or book they are writing about, state an opinion, supply reasons that support the opinion, use linking words (e.g., *because*, *and*, *also*) to connect opinion and reasons, and provide a concluding statement or section.

Math Activity 1.1: Measure Up!

K.MD.A.1 Describe measurable attributes of objects, such as length or weight. Describe several measurable attributes of a single object.

1.MD.A.1 Order three objects by length; compare the lengths of two objects indirectly by using a third object.

1.MD.A.2 Express the length of an object as a whole number of length units, by laying multiple copies of a shorter object (the length unit) end to end.

2.MD.A.1 Measure the length of an object by selecting and using appropriate tools such as rulers, yardsticks, meter sticks, and measuring tapes.

Chapter 2: It's Only Natural!

Introductory Activity 2.1: Natural vs. Man-Made

1-LS1 Structure and Function The shape and stability of structures of natural and designed objects are related to their function(s).

Science Activity 2.1: Sponge Power

2-PS1-1 Plan and conduct an investigation to describe and classify different kinds of materials by their observable properties.

Crosscutting Concept: Patterns Patterns in the natural and human designed world can be observed.

Science Activity 2.2: Nature Walk

1-LS1 Structure and Function The shape and stability of structures of natural and designed objects are related to their function(s).

ELA Activity 2.1: The Potter

RI.K.1 With prompting and support, ask and answer questions about key details in a text.

RI.1.1 Ask and answer questions about key details in a text.

RI.2.1 Ask and answer such questions as *who*, *what*, *where*, *when*, *why*, and *how* to demonstrate understanding of key details in a text.

RI.K.3 With prompting and support, describe the connection between two individuals, events, ideas, or pieces of information in a text.

RI.1.3 Describe the connection between two individuals, events, ideas, or pieces of information in a text.

Math Activity 2.1: Sponge Experiment Data

K-2.ETS1-3 Analyze data from tests of two objects designed to solve the same problem to compare the strengths and weaknesses of how each performs.

K.CC.C.6 Identify whether the number of objects in one group is greater than, less than, or equal to the number of objects in another group, e.g., by using matching and counting strategies.

1.NBT.B.3 Compare two two-digit numbers based on meanings of the tens and ones digits, recording the results of comparisons with the symbols >, =, and <.

2.NBT.A.4 Compare two three-digit numbers based on meanings of the hundreds, tens, and ones digits, using >, =, and < symbols to record the results of comparisons.

Math Activity 2.2: Nature Walk

K.MD.B.3 Classify objects into given categories; count the numbers of objects in each category and sort the categories by count.

Chapter 3: Natural Process

Introductory Activity 3.1: Natural Processes

1-LS1 Patterns Patterns in the natural and human designed world can be observed, used to describe phenomena, and used as evidence.

K-LS1-1 Use observations to describe patterns of what plants and animals (including humans) need to survive.

Science Activity 3.1: Sprouting Seeds

K-LS1-1 Use observations to describe patterns of what plants and animals (including humans) need to survive.

Science and Engineering Practices: Analyzing and Interpreting Data Analyzing data in K-2 builds on prior experiences and progresses to collecting, recording, and sharing observations.

Use observations to describe patterns in the natural world in order to answer scientific questions. (K-LS1-1)

ELA Activity 3.1: Creating Myths

RI.K.1 With prompting and support, ask and answer questions about key details in a text

RI.1.1 Ask and answer questions about key details in a text.

RI.2.1 Ask and answer such questions as *who*, *what*, *where*, *when*, *why*, and *how* to demonstrate understanding of key details in a text.

RI.K.3 With prompting and support, identify characters, settings, and major events in a story.

RI.1.3 Describe characters, settings, and major events in a story, using key details.

RI.K.7 With prompting and support, describe the relationship between illustrations and the story in which they appear (e.g., what person, place, thing, or idea in the text an illustration depicts).

RI.1.7 Use the illustration and details in a text to describe its key ideas.

RI.2.7 Explain how specific images (e.g., a diagram showing how a machine works) contribute to and clarify a text.

W.1.3 Write narratives in which they recount two or more appropriately sequenced events, include some details regarding what happened, use temporal words to signal event order, and provide some sense of closure.

W.2.3 Write narratives in which they recount a well-elaborated event or short sequence of events, include details to describe actions, thoughts, and feelings, use temporal words to signal event order, and provide a sense of closure.

Math Activity 3.1: Fractured Math

K.OA.A.2 Solve addition and subtraction word problems, and add and subtract within 10, e.g., by using objects or drawings to represent the problem.

1.OA.A.1 Use addition and subtraction within 20 to solve word problems involving situations of adding to, taking from, putting together, taking apart, and comparing, with unknowns in all positions, e.g., by using objects, drawings, and equations with a symbol for the unknown number to represent the problem.

2.OA.A.1 Use addition and subtraction within 100 to solve one- and two-step word problems involving situations of adding to, taking from, putting together, taking apart, and comparing, with unknowns in all positions, e.g., by using drawings and equations with a symbol for the unknown number to represent the problem.

Chapter 4: Be a Scientist!

Introductory Activity 4.1: The Role of a Scientist

K-2-ETS1 Ask questions, make observations, and gather information about a situation people want to change to define a simple problem that can be solved through the development of a new or improved object or tool.

Science Activity 4.1: Cleaning Up Dirt

K-PS3-1 Make observations to determine the effect of sunlight on Earth's surface.

Science and Engineering Practices: Planning and Carrying Out Investigations Planning and carrying out investigations to answer questions or test solutions to problems in K-2 builds on prior experiences and progresses to simple investigations, based on fair tests, which provide data to support explanations or design solutions. Make observations to collect data that can be used to make comparisons.

ELA Activity 4.1: What's the Big Idea?

RI.K.1 With prompting and support, ask and answer questions about key details in a text.

RI.1.1 Ask and answer questions about key details in a text.

RI.2.1 Ask and answer such questions as *who*, *what*, *where*, *when*, *why*, and *how* to demonstrate understanding of key details in a text.

RI.K.2 With prompting and support, identify the main topic and retell key details of a text.

RI.1.2 Identify the main topic and retell key details of a text.

RI.2.2 Identify the main topic of a multiparagraph text as well as the focus of specific paragraphs within the text.

RI.2.3 Describe the connection between a series of historical events, scientific ideas or concepts, or steps in technical procedures in a text.

RI.2.6 Identify the main purpose of a text, including what the author wants to answer, explain, or describe.

W.K.8 With guidance and support from adults, recall information from experiences or gather information from provided sources to answer a question.

W.1.8 With guidance and support from adults, recall information from experiences or gather information from provided sources to answer a question.

W.2.7 Participate in shared research and writing projects (e.g., read a number of books on a single topic to produce a report; record science observations).

Math Activity 4.1: Pizza Party!

K.OA.A.2 Solve addition and subtraction word problems, and add and subtract within 10, e.g., by using objects or drawings to represent the problem.

1.OA.A.2 Solve word problems that call for addition of three whole numbers whose sum is less than or equal to 20, e.g., by using objects, drawings, and equations with a symbol for the unknown number to represent the problem.

2.OA.C.4 Use addition to find the total number of objects arranged in rectangular arrays with up to 5 rows and up to 5 columns; write an equation to express the total as a sum of equal addends.

Unit Two: Physical Science

Chapter 5: What's the Matter?

Introductory Activity 5.1: Solids, Liquids, and Gases

2-PS1.A Different kinds of matter exist and many of them can be either solid or liquid, depending on temperature. Matter can be described and classified by its observable properties.

Science Activity 5.1: A Cool State of Matter and **Science Activity 5.2: Air Power** and **Science Activity 5.3: Bubble Science** and **Science Activity 5.4: Raising Raisins**

PS1.A Structure and Properties of Matter Different kinds of matter exist and many of them can be either solid or liquid, depending on temperature. Matter can be described and classified by its observable properties.

2-PS1-1 Plan and conduct an investigation to describe and classify different kinds of materials by their observable properties.

2-PS1-4 Construct an argument with evidence that some changes caused by heating or cooling can be reversed and some cannot.

2-PS1-2 Analyze data obtained from testing different materials to determine which materials have the properties that are best suited for an intended purpose.

2-PS1-3 Make observations to construct an evidence-based account of how an object made of a small set of pieces can be disassembled and made into a new object.

ELA Activity 5.1: Science Reporter

W.K.3 Use a combination of drawing, dictating, and writing to narrate a single event or several loosely linked events, tell about the events in the order in which they occurred, and provide a reaction to what happened.

W.1.3 Write narratives in which they recount two or more appropriately sequenced events, include some details regarding what happened, use temporal words to signal event order, and provide some sense of closure.

W.2.3 Write narratives in which they recount a well-elaborated event or short sequence of events, include details to describe actions, thoughts, and feelings, use temporal words to signal event order, and provide a sense of closure.

W.K.7 Participate in shared research and writing projects (e.g., explore a number of books by a favorite author and express opinions about them).

W.1.7 Participate in shared research and writing projects (e.g., explore a number of "how-to" books on a given topic and use them to write a sequence of instructions).

W.2.7 Participate in shared research and writing projects (e.g., read a number of books on a single topic to produce a report; record science observations).

Math Activity 5.1: Measuring Solids

K.MD.A.1 Describe measurable attributes of objects, such as length or weight. Describe several measurable attributes of a single object.

1.MD.A.1 Order three objects by length; compare the lengths of two objects indirectly by using a third object.

2.MD.A.1 Measure the length of an object by selecting and using appropriate tools such as rulers, yardsticks, meter sticks, and measuring tapes.

Chapter 6: Mixtures and Solutions

Introductory Activity 6.1: All Mixed Up!

2-PS1-1 Plan and conduct an investigation to describe and classify different kinds of materials by their observable properties.

2-PS1.A Different kinds of matter exist and many of them can be either solid or liquid, depending on temperature. Matter can be described and classified by its observable properties.

Science Activity 6.1: Exploration Stations

PS1.A Structure and Properties of Matter Different kinds of matter exist and many of them can be either solid or liquid, depending on temperature. Matter can be described and classified by its observable properties.

2-PS1-1 Plan and conduct an investigation to describe and classify different kinds of materials by their observable properties.

Science and Engineering Practices: Analyzing and Interpreting Data Analyzing data in K-2 builds on prior experiences and progresses to collecting, recording, and sharing observations.

ELA Activity 6.1: We've Got the Beat!

SL.K.2 Confirm understanding of a text read aloud or information presented orally or through other media by asking and answering questions about key details and requesting clarification if something is not understood.

L.K.6 Use words and phrases acquired through conversations, reading and being read to, and responding to texts.

RI.1.4 Use the illustrations and details in a text to describe its key ideas.

SL.1.2 Ask and answer questions about key details in a text read aloud or information presented orally or through other media.

SL.2.5 Create audio recordings of stories or poems; add drawings or other visual displays to stories or recounts of experiences when appropriate to clarify ideas, thoughts, and feelings.

RL.K.5 Recognize common types of texts (e.g., storybooks, poems).

Math Activity 6.1: Measuring Solutions and Mixtures

K.OA.A.1 Represent addition and subtraction with objects, fingers, mental images, drawings, sounds (e.g., claps), acting out situations, verbal explanations, expressions, or equations.

1.OA.A.1 and **2.OA.A.1** Use addition and subtraction within 100 to solve one- and two-step word problems involving situations of adding to, taking from, putting together, taking apart, and comparing, with unknowns in all positions, e.g., by using drawings and equations with a symbol for the unknown number to represent the problem.

Chapter 7: Mass and Falling Objects

Introductory Activity 7.1: Free Fall!

Science and Engineering Practices: Analyzing and Interpreting Data Analyzing data in K-2 builds on prior experiences and progresses to collecting, recording, and sharing observations. (K-PS2-1)

Science Activity 7.1: On Your Mark, Get Set, Go! and Science Activity 7.2: The Marble Challenge

PS2.A Forces and Motion Pushes and pulls can have different strengths and directions.

K.PS2-1 Plan and conduct an investigation to compare the effects of different strengths or different directions of pushes and pulls on the motion of an object.

K-PS2-2 Analyze data to determine if a design solution works as intended to change the speed or direction of an object with a push or a pull.

Science and Engineering Practices: Analyzing and Interpreting Data Analyzing data in K-2 builds on prior experiences and progresses to collecting, recording, and sharing observations.

ELA Activity 7.1 Sentence Cubes

L.K.1f Produce and expand complete sentences in shared language activities.

L.K.5b Demonstrate understanding of frequently occurring verbs and adjectives by relating them to their opposites (antonyms).

L.1.1j Produce and expand complete simple and compound declarative, interrogative, imperative, and exclamatory sentences in response to prompts.

L.1.1f Use frequently occurring adjectives.

L.2.1f Produce, expand, and rearrange complete simple and compound sentences.

L.2.1e Use adjectives and adverbs, and choose between them depending on what is to be modified.

Math Activity 7.1: Recording the Results of an Experiment

K.OA.A.2 Solve addition and subtraction word problems, and add and subtract within 10, e.g., by using objects or drawings to represent the problem.

1.OA.A.1 Use addition and subtraction within 20 to solve word problems involving situations of adding to, taking from, putting together, taking apart, and comparing, with unknowns in all positions, e.g., by using objects, drawings, and equations with a symbol for the unknown number to represent the problem.

2.OA.A.1 Use addition and subtraction within 100 to solve one- and two-step word problems involving situations of adding to, taking from, putting together, taking apart, and comparing, with unknowns in all positions, e.g., by using drawings and equations with a symbol for the unknown number to represent the problem.

Math Activity 7.2 Mathematical Symbols

K.MD.A.2 Directly compare two objects with a measurable attribute in common, to see which object has "more of"/"less of" the attribute, and describe the difference.

2.NBT.A.4 Compare two three-digit numbers based on meanings of the hundreds, tens, and ones digits, using >, =, and < symbols to record the results of comparisons.

1.NBT.B.3 Compare two two-digit numbers based on meanings of the tens and ones digits, recording the results of comparisons with the symbols >, =, and <.

1.MD.B.3 Tell and write time in hours and half-hours using analog and digital clocks.

2.MD.C.7 Tell and write time from analog and digital clocks to the nearest five minutes, using a.m. and p.m.

Chapter 8: Gravity

Introductory Activity 8.1: Newton's Apple

K-PS2-1 Science and Engineering Practices: Planning and Carrying Out Investigations With guidance, plan and conduct an investigation in collaboration with peers.

Science Activity 8.1: Egg Drop

K-2-ETS2 Develop a simple sketch, drawing, or physical model to illustrate how the shape of an object helps it function as needed to solve a given problem.

Science Activity 8.2: Impact!

K-PS2 Simple tests can be designed to gather evidence to support or refute student ideas about causes.

K.MD.A.2 Directly compare two objects with a measurable attribute in common, to see which object has "more of"/"less of" the attribute, and describe the difference.

1.MD.A.2 Express the length of an object as a whole number of length units, by laying multiple copies of a shorter object (the length unit) end to end; understand that the length measurement of an object is the number of same-size length units that span it with no gaps or overlaps.

2.MD.A.1 Measure the length of an object by selecting and using appropriate tools such as rulers, yardsticks, meter sticks, and measuring tapes.

ELA Activity 8.1: Just Imagine

L.K.4a Identify new meanings for familiar words and apply them accurately (e.g., knowing *duck* is a bird and learning the verb *to duck*).

L.K.5c Identify real-life connections between words and their use (e.g., note places at school that are colorful).

L.1.5 With guidance and support from adults, demonstrate understanding of word relationships and nuances in word meanings.

L.2.5a Identify real-life connections between words and their use (e.g., *describe foods that are spicy or juicy*).

Math Activity 8.1: Equation and Balance

2.OA.C.4 Use addition to find the total number of objects arranged in rectangular arrays with up to 5 rows and up to 5 columns; write an equation to express the total as a sum of equal addends.

1.OA.D.7 Understand the meaning of the equal sign, and determine if equations involving addition and subtraction are true or false.

K.OA.A.3 Decompose numbers less than or equal to 10 into pairs in more than one way, e.g., by using objects or drawings, and record each decomposition by a drawing or equation (e.g., 5 = 2 + 3 and 5 = 4 + 1).

Chapter 9: Motion, Force, and Energy

Introductory Activity 9.1: Get Energized!

K-PS2-1 Plan and conduct an investigation to compare the effects of different strengths or different directions of pushes and pulls on the motion of an object.

Science Activity 9.1: Domino Trains

PS2.A Forces and Motion Pushes and pulls can have different strengths and directions. Pushing or pulling on an object can change the speed or direction of its motion and can start or stop it.

K-PS2-1 Plan and conduct an investigation to compare the effects of different strengths or different directions of pushes and pulls on the motion of an object.

K-PS2-2 Analyze data to determine if a design solution works as intended to change the speed or direction of an object with a push or a pull.

PS2.B Types of interactions When objects touch or collide, they push on one another and can change motion.

PS3.C Relationship Between Energy and Forces A bigger push or pull makes things go faster.

Science Activity 9.2: The Need for Speed

K-PS2-2 Analyze data to determine if a design solution works as intended to change the speed or direction of an object with a push or pull.

ETS1A Defining Engineering Problems A situation that people want to change or create can be approached as a problem to be solved through engineering. Such problems may have many acceptable solutions.

1.MD.B.3 Tell and write time in hours and half-hours using analog and digital clocks.

2.MD.C.7 Tell and write time from analog and digital clocks to the nearest five minutes, using a.m. and p.m.

ELA Activity 9.1 What Do You Know?

W.K-2.8 With guidance and support from adults, recall information from experiences or gather information from provided sources to answer a question.

Math Activity 9.1: Domino Math

Math Activity 9.2 Advanced Domino Math

K.CC.C.6 Identify whether the number of objects in one group is greater than, less than, or equal to the number of objects in another group, e.g., by using matching and counting strategies.

1.OA.A.1 / 2.OA.A.1 Use addition and subtraction within 100 to solve one- and two-step word problems involving situations of adding to, taking from, putting together, taking apart, and comparing, with unknowns in all positions.

Chapter 10: Simple Machines

Introductory Activity 10.1: This is a Job for . . . Simple Machines

K-2-ETS1.A A situation that people want to change or create can be approached as a problem to be solved through engineering.

Science Activity 10.1: Cotton Ball Catapult

K-PS2-2 Analyze data to determine if a design solution works as intended to change the speed or direction of an object with a push or a pull.

K-PS2.A Forces and Motion Pushes and pulls can have different strengths and directions.

ETSA1.A Defining Engineering Problems A situation that people want to change or create can be approached as a problem to be solved through engineering.

Science and Engineering Practices: Analyzing Data Analyze data from tests of an object or tool to determine if it works as intended.

1.MD.A.2 Express the length of an object as a whole number of length units, by laying multiple copies of a shorter object (the length unit) end to end.

2.MD.A.3 Estimate lengths using units of inches, feet, centimeters, and meters.

Science Activity 10.2: Raise the Flag

K-PS2-2 Analyze data to determine if a design solution works as intended to change the speed or direction of an object with a push or a pull.

ETSA1.A Defining Engineering Problems A situation that people want to change or create can be approached as a problem to be solved through engineering.

Science and Engineering Practices: Analyzing Data Analyze data from tests of an object or tool to determine if it works as intended.

Science Activity 10.3: Name That Simple Machine

PS2.A Forces and Motion. Pushes and pulls can have different strengths and directions.

ELA Activity 10.1: The Twiddles

W.K.3 Use a combination of drawing, dictating, and writing to narrate a single event or several loosely linked events, tell about the events in the order in which they occurred, and provide a reaction to what happened.

W.1.3 Write narratives in which they recount two or more appropriately sequenced events, include some details regarding what happened, use temporal words to signal event order, and provide some sense of closure.

W.2.3 Write narratives in which they recount a well-elaborated event or short sequence of events, include details to describe actions, thoughts, and feelings, use temporal words to signal event order, and provide a sense of closure.

Math Activity 10.1: Cotton Ball Math

K.NBT.A.1 Compose and decompose numbers from 11 to 19 into ten ones and some further ones, e.g., by using objects or drawings, and record each composition or decomposition by a drawing or equation.

1.OA.A.1 Use addition and subtraction within 20 to solve word problems involving situations of adding to, taking from, putting together, taking apart, and comparing, with unknowns in all positions.

2.NBT.B.5 Fluently add and subtract within 100 using strategies based on place value, properties of operations, and/or the relationship between addition and subtraction.

Chapter 11: Magnetic Attraction

Introductory Activity 11.1: It's Magnetic!

K-PS2 Plan and conduct an investigation to compare the effects of different strengths or different directions of pushes and pulls on the motion of an object.

Science Activity 11.1: Sandbox Discovery

ELA.L.K.5a Sort common objects into categories (e.g., shapes, foods) to gain a sense of the concepts the categories represent.

Science Activity 11.2 Go Fly a Kite!

K-PS2-1 Plan and conduct an investigation to compare the effects of different strengths or different directions of pushes and pulls on the motion of an object.

2-PS1-1 Plan and conduct an investigation to describe and classify different kinds of materials by their observable properties.

Science and Engineering Practices: Science Models, Laws, Mechanisms, and Theories Explain Natural Phenomena Scientists search for cause and effect relationships to explain natural events. (2-PS1-4)

ELA Activity 11.1: Spill and Spell

L.K-2.1 Demonstrate command of the conventions of standard English capitalization, punctuation, and spelling when writing.

L.K.2d Spell simple words phonetically, drawing on knowledge of sound-letter relationships.

L.1.2d Use conventional spelling for words with common spelling patterns and for frequently occurring irregular words.

Math Activity 11.1: Fishing for Math with Magnets

K.OA.A.1 Represent addition and subtraction with objects, fingers, mental images, drawings, sounds (e.g., claps), acting out situations, verbal explanations, expressions, or equations.

1.OA.B.3 Apply properties of operations as strategies to add and subtract.

2.OA.A.1 Use addition and subtraction within 100 to solve one- and two-step word problems involving situations of adding to, taking from, putting together, taking apart, and comparing, with unknowns in all positions.

Unit Three: Earth and Space Science

Chapter 12: Patterns of the Earth, Moon, and Sun

Introductory Activity 12.1: Day After Day: Natural Patterns in Space

1-ESS1 Use observations of the sun, moon, and stars to describe patterns that can be predicted.

Science Activity 12.1: Gravity and Earth's Rotation and Science Activity 12.2: The Moon's Rotation Around Earth and Science Activity 12.3: Sun Dial

ESS1.A The Universe and its Stars Patterns of the motion of the sun, moon, and stars in the sky can be observed, described, and predicted.

1-ESS1-1 Use observations of the sun, moon, and stars to describe patterns that can be predicted.

ESS1.B Earth and the Solar System - Seasonal patterns of sunrise and sunset can be observed, described, and predicted.

Science and Engineering Practices: Analyzing and Interpreting Data Analyzing data in K-2 builds on prior experiences and progresses to collecting, recording, and sharing observations. Use observations to describe patterns in the natural world in order to answer scientific questions. (1-ESS1-1)

ELA Activity 12.1: The Man in the Moon

W.K.3 Use a combination of drawing, dictating, and writing to narrate a single event or several loosely linked events, tell about the events in the order in which they occurred, and provide a reaction to what happened.

W.1.3 Write narratives in which they recount two or more appropriately sequenced events, include some details regarding what happened, use temporal words to signal event order, and provide some sense of closure.

W.2.3 Write narratives in which they recount a well-elaborated event or short sequence of events, include details to describe actions, thoughts, and feelings, use temporal words to signal event order, and provide a sense of closure.

L.K-2.2 Use knowledge of language and its conventions when writing, speaking, reading, or listening.

Math Activity 12.1: Fly to the Moon

2.OA.A.1 Use addition and subtraction within 100 to solve one- and two-step word problems involving situations of adding to, taking from, putting together, taking apart, and comparing, with unknowns in all positions.

1.OA.B.3 Apply properties of operations as strategies to add and subtract.

K.OA.A.3 Decompose numbers less than or equal to 10 into pairs in more than one way, e.g., by using objects or drawings, and record each decomposition by a drawing or equation (e.g., $5 = 2 + 3$ and $5 = 4 + 1$).

K.OA.A.4 For any number from 1 to 9, find the number that makes 10 when added to the given number, e.g., by using objects or drawings, and record the answer with a drawing or equation.

Chapter 13: Properties of the Sun

Introductory Activity 13.1: Heat Wave!

K-PS3-1 Make observations to determine the effect of sunlight on Earth's surface.

Science Activity 13.1: The Power of the Sun and **Science Activity 13.2: Melting Ice**

Crosscutting Concepts: Cause and Effect Simple tests can be designed to gather evidence to support or refute student ideas about causes. (2-PS1-2)

K-PS3-2 Use tools and materials to design and build a structure that will reduce the warming effect of sunlight on an area.

PS3.B Conservation of Energy and Energy Transfer Sunlight warms Earth's surface.

ELA Activity 13.1: It's in the Air

ESS3.C Human Impacts on Earth Systems Things that people do to live comfortably can affect the world around them. But they can make choices that reduce their impacts on the land, water, air, and other living things.

ETS1.A Defining and Delimiting Engineering Problems A situation that people want to change or create can be approached as a problem to be solved through engineering.

W.K.2 Use a combination of drawing, dictating, and writing to compose informative/explanatory texts in which they name what they are writing about and supply some information about the topic.

W.1.2 Write informative/explanatory texts in which they name a topic, supply some facts about the topic, and provide some sense of closure.

W.2.2 Write informative/explanatory texts in which they introduce a topic, use facts and definitions to develop points, and provide a concluding statement or section.

W.K.8 With guidance and support from adults, recall information from experiences or gather information from provided sources to answer a question.

W.1.8 With guidance and support from adults, recall information from experiences or gather information from provided sources to answer a question.

W.2.8 Recall information from experiences or gather information from provided sources to answer a question.

Math Activity 13.1: Air Pollution Pie Chart

1.MD.C.4 Organize, represent, and interpret data with up to three categories; ask and answer questions about the total number of data points, how many in each category, and how many more or less are in one category than in another.

MD.D.10 Draw a picture graph and a bar graph (with single-unit scale) to represent a data set with up to four categories.

Chapter 14: The Water Cycle

Introductory Activity 14.1: Today's Weather Forecast

K-PS3 Make observation to determine the effect of sunlight on Earth's surface.

K-PS3.B Sunlight warms Earth's surface.

K-ESS2-1.D Weather is the combination of sunlight, wind, snow or rain, and temperature in a particular region at a particular time. People measure these conditions to describe and record the weather and to notice patterns over time.

RI.K.7 With prompting and support, describe the relationship between illustrations and the text in which they appear (e.g., what person, place, thing, or idea in the text an illustration depicts).

RI.1.7 Use the illustrations and details in a text to describe its key ideas.

RI.2.7 Explain how specific images (e.g., a diagram showing how a machine works) contribute to and clarify a text.

Science Activity 14.1: Bottled Water

K-PS3-1 Make observations to determine the effect of sunlight on Earth's surface.

Science Activity 14.2: Clouds in a Cup

ESS3.A Natural Resources Living things need water, air, and resources from the land, and they live in places that have the things they need. Humans use natural resources for everything they do.

Science Activity 14.3: Rain Clouds

Science and Engineering: Developing and Using Models Use a model to represent relationships in the natural world. (I-ESS3)

ELA Activity 14.1: Letter Drop

L.1.2d Use conventional spelling for words with common spelling patterns and for frequently occurring irregular words.

L.2.2d Generalize learned spelling patterns when writing words (e.g., *cage, badge; boy, boil*).

Math Activity 14.1: Rain Gauge

K.OA.A.1 Represent addition and subtraction with objects, fingers, mental images, drawings, sounds (e.g., claps), acting out situations, verbal explanations, expressions, or equations.

1.NBT.A.1 Count to 120, starting at any number less than 120. In this range, read and write numerals and represent a number of objects with a written numeral.

2.NBT.A.2 Count within 1000; skip-count by 5s, 10s, and 100s.

K.CC.A.2 Count forward beginning from a given number within the known sequence (instead of having to begin at 1).

Chapter 15: Rocks and the Weather

Introductory Activity 15.1: World of Rocks

2-ESS1.C Some events happen very quickly; others occur very slowly, over a time period much longer than one can observe.

2-ESS2.A Earth materials and systems Wind and water can change the shape of the land.

Science Activity 15.1: Rock Formation

2-ESS2.A Earth materials and systems - Wind and water can change the shape of the land.

ELA Activity 15.1: Describe It

L.K.5b Demonstrate understanding of frequently occurring verbs and adjectives by relating them to their opposites (antonyms).

L.2.1e Use adjectives and adverbs, and choose between them depending on what is to be modified.

L.1.1f Use frequently occurring adjectives.

Math Activity 15.1: Math Rocks!

K.OA.A.2 Solve addition and subtraction word problems, and add and subtract within 10, e.g., by using objects or drawings to represent the problem.

1.OA.A.1 Use addition and subtraction within 20 to solve word problems involving situations of adding to, taking from, putting together, taking apart, and comparing, with unknowns in all positions.

2.OA.A.1 Use addition and subtraction within 100 to solve one- and two-step word problems involving situations of adding to, taking from, putting together, taking apart, and comparing, with unknowns in all positions.

Chapter 16: The Layers of the Earth

Introductory Activity 16.1: If the Earth Were an Apple

Science and Engineering Practices: Developing and Using Models Use a model to represent relationships in the natural world. (K-ESS3-1)

Science Activity 16.1: Earth Model

ETS1.B Developing Possible Solutions Designs can be conveyed through sketches, drawings, or physical models.

Science Activity 16.2: The Density of Earth's Layers

PS1.A Structure and Properties of Matter Different kinds of matter exist and many of them can be either solid or liquid, depending on temperature. Matter can be described and classified by its observable properties. A great variety of objects can be built up from a small set of pieces.

2-ESS2.B Plate Tectonics and Large-Scale System Interactions

ELA Activity 16.1: Getting to the Core

RF.K.1b Recognize that spoken words are represented in written language by specific sequences of letters.

RF.K.3d Distinguish between similarly spelled words by identifying the sounds of the letters that differ.

L.K.6 Use words and phrases acquired through conversations, reading and being read to, and responding to texts.

L.1.6 Use words and phrases acquired through conversations, reading and being read to, and responding to texts.

L.2.2d Generalize learned spelling patterns when writing words (e.g., *cage, badge*; *boy, boil*).

Math Activity 16.1: It's Hot!

K.CC.B.4c Understand that each successive number name refers to a quantity that is one larger.

1.MD.C.4 Organize, represent, and interpret data with up to three categories; ask and answer questions about the total number of data points, how many in each category, and how many more or less are in one category than in another.

2.MD.D.10 Draw a picture graph and a bar graph (with single-unit scale) to represent a data set with up to four categories. Solve simple put-together, take-apart, and compare problems using information presented in a bar graph.

Chapter 17: Earthquakes and Volcanoes

Introductory Activity 17.1: Shaky Ground

1-ESS1-1: Patterns Patterns in the natural world can be observed, used to describe phenomena, and used as evidence.

K.G.B.5 Model shapes in the world by building shapes from components (e.g., sticks and clay balls) and drawing shapes.

1.G.A.3 Partition circles and rectangles into two and four equal shares, describe the shares using the words *halves*, *fourths*, and *quarters*, and use the phrases *half of*, *fourth of*, and *quarter of*. Describe the whole as two of, or four of, the shares.

2.G.A.3 Partition circles and rectangles into two, three, or four equal shares, describe the shares using the words halves, thirds, half of, a third of, etc., and describe the whole as two halves, three thirds, four fourths.

Science Activity 17.1: Volcano! and Science Activity 17.2: It's a Blast!

2-ESS1-1 Make observations from media to construct an evidence-based account that Earth events can occur quickly or slowly.

Science and Engineering Practices: Developing and Using Models Use a model to represent relationships in the natural world. Make observations to collect data that can be used to make comparisons.

1-ESS1-1: Patterns Patterns in the natural world can be observed, used to describe phenomena, and used as evidence.

Science Activity 17.3: Earthquake!

2-ESS1-1 Make observations from media to construct an evidence-based account that Earth events can occur quickly or slowly.

Science and Engineering Practices: Developing and Using Models Use a model to represent relationships in the natural world. Make observations to collect data that can be used to make comparisons.

ELA Activity 17.1: Plurals Add Up!

L.K.1c Form regular plural nouns orally by adding /s/ or /es/ (e.g., *dog*, *dogs*; *wish*, *wishes*).

L.1.2d Use conventional spelling for words with common spelling patterns and for frequently occurring irregular words.

L.2.2 Demonstrate command of the conventions of standard English capitalization, punctuation, and spelling when writing.

K.OA.A.2 Solve addition and subtraction word problems, and add and subtract within 10, e.g., by using objects or drawings to represent the problem.

K.OA.A.5 Fluently add and subtract within 5.

1.OA.B.3 Apply properties of operations as strategies to add and subtract.

1.OA.A.1 Use addition and subtraction within 20 to solve word problems involving situations of adding to, taking from, putting together, taking apart, and comparing, with unknowns in all positions.

2.OA.A.1 Use addition and subtraction within 100 to solve one- and two-step word problems involving situations of adding to, taking from, putting together, taking apart, and comparing, with unknowns in all positions.

ELA Activity 17.2: Foldable Volcano Eruption

W.K.2 Use a combination of drawing, dictating, and writing to compose informative/explanatory texts in which they name what they are writing about and supply some information about the topic.

W.1.2 Write informative/explanatory texts in which they name a topic, supply some facts about the topic, and provide some sense of closure.

W.2.2 Write informative/explanatory texts in which they introduce a topic, use facts and definitions to develop points, and provide a concluding statement or section.

SL.K.5 Add drawings or other visual displays to descriptions as desired to provide additional detail.

SL.1.5 Add drawings or other visual displays to descriptions when appropriate to clarify ideas, thoughts, and feelings.

SL.2.5 Create audio recordings of stories or poems; add drawings or other visual displays to stories or recounts of experiences when appropriate to clarify ideas, thoughts, and feelings.

Math Activity 17.1: Get Quaking!

K.CC.A.1 Count to 100 by ones and by tens.

1.NBT.A.1 Count to 120, starting at any number less than 120. In this range, read and write numerals and represent a number of objects with a written numeral.

Chapter 18: The Rock Cycle

Introductory Activity 18.1: The Rocky Road of the Rock Cycle

2-ESS1 Use information from several sources to provide evidence that Earth events can occur quickly or slowly.

2-ESS2.A Wind and water can change the shape of the land.

Science Activity 18.1: The Changing State of Rocks

ESS1.C The History of Planet Earth Some events happen very quickly; others occur very slowly, over a time period much longer than one can observe.

2-PS1-1 Plan and conduct an investigation to describe and classify different kinds of materials by their observable properties.

Science and Engineering Practices: Obtaining, Evaluating, and Communicating Information Ask questions based on observations to find more information about the natural and/or designed world(s).

ELA Activity 18.1: Rock Star

W.K.3 Use a combination of drawing, dictating, and writing to narrate a single event or several loosely linked events, tell about the events in the order in which they occurred, and provide a reaction to what happened.

W.1.3 Write narratives in which they recount two or more appropriately sequenced events, include some details regarding what happened, use temporal words to signal event order, and provide some sense of closure.

W.2.3 Write narratives in which they recount a well-elaborated event or short sequence of events, include details to describe actions, thoughts, and feelings, use temporal words to signal event order, and provide a sense of closure.

Math Activity 18.1: Rock Swap

1.OA.B.3 Apply properties of operations as strategies to add and subtract.

K.OA.A.1 Represent addition and subtraction with objects, fingers, mental images, drawings, sounds (e.g., claps), acting out situations, verbal explanations, expressions, or equations.

2.OA.A.1 Use addition and subtraction within 100 to solve one- and two-step word problems involving situations of adding to, taking from, putting together, taking apart, and comparing, with unknowns in all positions.

Chapter 19: Soil

Introductory Activity 19.1: When Soil Breaks Down

2-LS4.D There are many different kinds of living things in any area, and they exist in different places on land and in water.

Science Activity 19.1: What's in Your Soil?

Activity 19.2: Soil Mixtures and Plant Growth

LS1.C Organization for Matter and Energy Flow in Organisms All animals need food in order to live and grow. They obtain their food from plants or from other animals. Plants need water and light to live and grow.

ESS3.A Natural Resources Living things need water, air, and resources from the land, and they live in places that have the things they need. Humans use natural resources for everything they do.

K-LS1-1 Use observations to describe patterns of what plants and animals (including humans) need to survive.

ELA Activity 19.1: Plant Growth Interpretation

W.K.2 Use a combination of drawing, dictating, and writing to compose informative/explanatory texts in which they name what they are writing about and supply some information about the topic.

W.K.7 Participate in shared research and writing projects (e.g., explore a number of books by a favorite author and express opinions about them).

W.1.2 Write informative/explanatory texts in which they name a topic, supply some facts about the topic, and provide some sense of closure.

W.1.7 Participate in shared research and writing projects (e.g., explore a number of "how-to" books on a given topic and use them to write a sequence of instructions).

W.2.2 Write informative/explanatory texts in which they introduce a topic, use facts and definitions to develop points, and provide a concluding statement or section.

W.2.7 Participate in shared research and writing projects (e.g., read a number of books on a single topic to produce a report; record science observations).

Math Activity 19.1: Break it Down!

K.NBT.A.1 Compose and decompose numbers from 11 to 19 into ten ones and some further ones.

1.NBT.B.2 Understand that the two digits of a two-digit number represent amounts of tens and ones.

2.NBT.A.1 Understand that the three digits of a three-digit number represent amounts of hundreds, tens, and ones; e.g., 706 equals 7 hundreds, 0 tens, and 6 ones.

Chapter 20: Reduce, Reuse, Recycle

Introductory Activity 20.1: Reduce: Trash Piles and Pollution

K-ESS3.C Things that people do to live comfortably can affect the world around them. But they can make choices that reduce their impact on the land, water, air, and other living things.

Science Activity 20.1: Reuse: Terrarium and **Science Activity 20.2: Recycle: Paper**

K-ESS3-3 Communicate solutions that will reduce the impact of humans on the land, water, air, and/or other living things in the local environment.

ESS3.A Natural Resources Living things need water, air, and resources from the land, and they live in places that have the things they need. Humans use natural resources for everything they do.

ESS3.C Human Impacts on Earth Systems Things that people do to live comfortably can affect the world around them. But they can make choices that reduce their impacts on the land, water, air, and other living things.

ETS1.A Defining and Delimiting Engineering Problems A situation that people want to change or create can be approached as a problem to be solved through engineering. Asking questions, making observations, and gathering information are helpful in thinking about problems.

ETS1.B Developing Possible Solutions Designs can be conveyed through sketches, drawings, or physical models. These representations are useful in communicating ideas for a problem's solutions to other people.

LS2.A Interdependent Relationships in Ecosystems Plants depend on water and light to grow.

ELA Activity 20.1: Quiet on the Set!

W.K.3 Use a combination of drawing, dictating, and writing to narrate a single event or several loosely linked events, tell about the events in the order in which they occurred, and provide a reaction to what happened.

W.1.3 Write narratives in which they recount two or more appropriately sequenced events, include some details regarding what happened, use temporal words to signal event order, and provide some sense of closure.

W.2.3 Write narratives in which they recount a well-elaborated event or short sequence of events, include details to describe actions, thoughts, and feelings, use temporal words to signal event order, and provide a sense of closure.

L.K.2 Demonstrate command of the conventions of standard English capitalization, punctuation, and spelling when writing.

L.1.2 Demonstrate command of the conventions of standard English capitalization, punctuation, and spelling when writing.

L.2.2 Demonstrate command of the conventions of standard English capitalization, punctuation, and spelling when writing.

Math Activity 20.1: Bottle Cap Math

K.CC.B.4c Understand that each successive number name refers to a quantity that is one larger.

K.MD.A.2 Directly compare two objects with a measurable attribute in common, to see which object has "more of"/"less of" the attribute, and describe the difference.

1.NBT.B.2 Understand that the two digits of a two-digit number represent amounts of tens and ones.

2.NBT.A.1 Understand that the three digits of a three-digit number represent amounts of hundreds, tens, and ones; e.g., 706 equals 7 hundreds, 0 tens, and 6 ones.

2.OA.C.4 Use addition to find the total number of objects arranged in rectangular arrays with up to 5 rows and up to 5 columns; write an equation to express the total as a sum of equal addends.

Activity 20.2: More Bottle Cap Math

2.OA.C.4 Use addition to find the total number of objects arranged in rectangular arrays with up to 5 rows and up to 5 columns; write an equation to express the total as a sum of equal addends.

Unit Four: Life Science

Chapter 21: Food Chains

Introductory Activity 21.1: What's for Lunch?

K-LS1.C Organization for Matter and Energy Flow in Organisms All animals need food in order to live and grow. They obtain their food from plants or from other animals. Plants need water and light to live and grow.

Science Activity 21.1: Fishing for a Food Chain

K-LS1-1 Use observations to describe patterns of what plants and animals (including humans) need to survive.

K-LS1-C Organization for Matter and Energy Flow in Organisms All animals need food in order to live and grow. They obtain their food from plants or from other animals. Plants need water and light to live and grow.

K-ESS3-1 Use a model to represent the relationship between the needs of different plants or animals (including humans).

ETS1-B Developing Possible Solutions Designs can be conveyed through sketches, drawings, or physical models. The representations are useful in communicating ideas for a problem's solutions to other people.

Science Activity 21.2: Who's Hungry?

LS1.C Organization for Matter and Energy Flow in Organisms.

ELA Activity 21.1: Diving Deeper

W.K-2.8 With guidance and support from adults, recall information from experiences or gather information from provided sources to answer a question.

Math Activity 21.1: Life Span Bar Graph

K.MD.A.2 Directly compare two objects with a measurable attribute in common, to see which object has "more of"/"less of" the attribute, and describe the difference.

1.MD.C.4 Organize, represent, and interpret data with up to three categories; ask and answer questions about the total number of data points, how many in each category, and how many more or less are in one category than in another.

2.MD.D.10 Draw a picture graph and a bar graph (with single-unit scale) to represent a data set with up to four categories.

Chapter 22: Habitats and Ecosystems

Introductory Activity 22.1: At Home in a Habitat

2-LS4-1 Make observations of plants and animals to compare the diversity of life in different habitats.

2-LS2.A Plants depend on water and light to grow.

Science Activity 22.1: Create an Ecosystem

2-LS4-1 Make observations of plants and animals to compare the diversity of life in different habitats.

K-ESS3-1 Use a model to represent the relationship between the needs of different plants or animals (including humans) and the places they live.

Science and Engineering Practices: Obtaining, Evaluating, and Communicating Information Obtaining, evaluating, and communicating information in K-2 builds on prior experiences and uses observations and texts to communicate new information. (1-LS1-2)

ELA Activity 22.1: Save Our Animals

W.K.1 Use a combination of drawing, dictating, and writing to compose opinion pieces in which they tell a reader the topic or the name of the book they are writing about and state an opinion or preference about the topic or book.

W.1.1 Write opinion pieces in which they introduce the topic or name the book they are writing about, state an opinion, supply a reason for the opinion, and provide some sense of closure.

W.2.1 Write opinion pieces in which they introduce the topic or book they are writing about, state an opinion, supply reasons that support the opinion, use linking words (e.g., *because*, *and*, *also*) to connect opinion and reasons, and provide a concluding statement or section.

Math Activity 22.1: Endangered Species

1.NBT.B.3 Compare two two-digit numbers based on meanings of the tens and ones digits, recording the results of comparisons with the symbols >, =, and <.

2.NBT.A.1 Understand that the three digits of a three-digit number represent amounts of hundreds, tens, and ones; e.g., 706 equals 7 hundreds, 0 tens, and 6 ones.

2.NBT.A.3 Read and write numbers to 1000 using base-ten numerals, number names, and expanded form.

2.NBT.B.7 Add and subtract within 1000, using concrete models or drawings and strategies based on place value, properties of operations, and/or the relationship between addition and subtraction; relate the strategy to a written method.

Chapter 23: The Five Senses

Introductory Activity 23.1: Sensing Danger

1-LS1-A All organisms have external parts. Different animals use their body parts in different ways to see, hear, grasp objects, protect themselves, move from place to place, and seek, find, and take in food, water and air.

Science Activity 23.1: Taste Test 1: Sight and Taste and **Science Activity 23.2: Taste Test 2: Smell and Taste**

LS1.D Information Processing Animals have body parts that capture and convey different kinds of information needed for growth and survival. Animals respond to these inputs with behaviors that help them survive. Plants also respond to some external inputs.

LS1.A Structure and Functions All organisms have external parts. Different animals use their body parts in different ways to see, hear, grasp objects, protect themselves, move from place to place, and seek, find, and take in food, water and air. Plants also have different parts (roots, stems, leaves, flowers, fruits) that help them survive and grow.

Science Activity 23.3: Sound Waves 1: Vibrating Rice and **Science Activity 23.4: Sound Waves 2: Musical Vibes**

1-PS4-1 Plan and conduct investigations to provide evidence that vibrating materials can make sound and that sound can make materials vibrate.

1-PS4.A Wave Properties Sound can make matter vibrate, and vibrating matter can make sound.

Science Activity 23.5: Match Up 1: Touch and **Science Activity 23.6: Match Up 2: Smell**

LS1.A Structure and Functions All organisms have external parts. Different animals use their body parts in different ways to see, hear, grasp objects, protect themselves, move from place to place, and seek, find, and take in food, water and air. Plants also have different parts (roots, stems, leaves, flowers, fruits) that help them survive and grow.

ELA Activity 23.1: Sounds Like

RF.K.1b Recognize that spoken words are represented in written language by specific sequences of letters.

RF.K.2 Demonstrate understanding of spoken words, syllables, and sounds (phonemes).

RF.1.2 Demonstrate understanding of spoken words, syllables, and sounds (phonemes).

L.K.5a Sort common objects into categories (e.g., shapes, foods) to gain a sense of the concepts the categories represent.

L.1.5a Sort words into categories (e.g., colors, clothing) to gain a sense of the concepts the categories represent.

L.2.5a Identify real-life connections between words and their use (e.g., *describe foods that are spicy or juicy*).

Math Activity 23.1: Thunderstorm

K.CC.A.2 Count forward beginning from a given number within the known sequence (instead of having to begin at 1).

1.NBT.A.1 Count to 120, starting at any number less than 120. In this range, read and write numerals and represent a number of objects with a written numeral.

2.NBT.A.2 Count within 1000; skip-count by 5s, 10s, and 100s.

Chapter 24: Vertebrates and Invertebrates

Introductory Activity 24.1: Classifying Organisms

1-LS3.A Young animals are very much, but not exactly like, their parents.

1-LS1.A All organisms have external parts. Different animals use their body parts in different ways to see, hear, grasp objects, protect themselves, move from place to place, and seek, find, and take in food, water and air.

1-LS1.D Animals have body parts that capture and convey different kinds of information needed for growth and survival.

Science Activity 24.1: Vertebrae on a Human Spine and **Science Activity 24.2: An Invertebrate Model: Jellyfish**

1-LS3-1 Make observations to construct an evidence-based account that young plants and animals are like, but not exactly like, their parents.

LS3.B Variation of Traits Individuals of the same kind of plant or animal are recognizable as similar but can also vary in many ways.

LS3.A Inheritance of Traits Young animals are very much, but not exactly, like their parents. Plants also are very much, but not exactly, like their parents.

K-ESS3-1 Use a model to represent the relationship between the needs of different plants or animals (including humans) and the places they live.

ESS3.A Natural Resources Living things need water, air, and resources from the land, and they live in places that have the things they need. Humans use natural resources for everything they do.

Science and Engineering Practices: Developing and Using Models Modeling in K-2 builds on prior experiences and progresses to include using and developing models that represent concrete events or design solutions. Use a model to represent patterns in the natural world. (2-ESS2-2)

ELA Activity 24.1: New at the Zoo

SL.K.5 Add drawings or other visual displays to descriptions as desired to provide additional detail.

SL.1.5 Add drawings or other visual displays to descriptions when appropriate to clarify ideas, thoughts, and feelings.

SL.2.5 Create audio recordings of stories or poems; add drawings or other visual displays to stories or recounts of experiences when appropriate to clarify ideas, thoughts, and feelings.

SL.K-1.4 Describe people, places, things, and events with relevant details, expressing ideas and feelings clearly.

RI.1.7 Use illustrations and details in a text to describe its key ideas.

Math Activity 24.1: Math Bones

K.OA.A.1 Represent addition and subtraction with objects, fingers, mental images, drawings, sounds (e.g., claps), acting out situations, verbal explanations, expressions, or equations.

1.OA.B.3 Apply properties of operations as strategies to add and subtract.

2.OA.A.1 Use addition and subtraction within 100 to solve one- and two-step word problems involving situations of adding to, taking from, putting together, taking apart, and comparing, with unknowns in all positions.

Chapter 25: Life Cycles

Introductory Activity: The Stages of Life

1-LS1.B Adult plants and animals can have young. In many kinds of animals, parents and the offspring themselves engage in behaviors that help the offspring to survive.

Science: Activity 25.1: Life Cycle of a Butterfly

Activity 25.2: Potato Garden

LS1.C Organization for Matter and Energy Flow in Organisms All animals need food in order to live and grow. They obtain their food from plants or from other animals. Plants need water and light to live and grow.

ESS3.A Natural Resources Living things need water, air, and resources from the land, and they live in places that have the things they need. Humans use natural resources for everything they do.

LS1.B Growth and Development of Organisms Adult plants and animals can have young. In many kinds of animals, parents and the offspring themselves engage in behaviors that help the offspring to survive.

LS3.B Variation of Traits Individuals of the same kind of plant or animal are recognizable as similar but can also vary in many ways.

Science and Engineering Practices: Planning and Carrying Out Investigations Planning and carrying out investigations to answer questions or test solutions to problems in K-2 builds on prior experiences and progresses to simple investigations, based on fair tests, which provide data to support explanations or design solutions. Make observations to collect data which can be used to make comparisons. (2-LS4-1)

ELA Activity 25.1: Circles of Life

RI.K.3 With prompting and support, describe the connection between two individuals, events, ideas, or pieces of information in a text.

RI.1.3 Describe the connection between two individuals, events, ideas, or pieces of information in a text.

RI.2.9 Compare and contrast the most important points presented by two texts on the same topic.

W.K.1 Use a combination of drawing, dictating, and writing to compose informative/explanatory texts in which they name what they are writing about and supply some information about the topic.

1.OA.A.1 Use addition and subtraction within 20 to solve word problems involving situations of adding to, taking from, putting together, taking apart, and comparing, with unknowns in all positions, supply some facts about the topic, and provide some sense of closure.

W.2.2 Write informative/explanatory texts in which they introduce a topic, use facts and definitions to develop points, and provide a concluding statement or section.

Math Activity 25.1: What's Up at the Zoo?

K.CC.B.4 Understand the relationship between numbers and quantities; connect counting to cardinality.

1.OA.A.1 Use addition and subtraction within 20 to solve word problems involving situations of adding to, taking from, putting together, taking apart, and comparing, with unknowns in all positions, supply some facts about the topic, and provide some sense of closure.

2.OA.A.1 Use addition and subtraction within 100 to solve one- and two-step word problems involving situations of adding to, taking from, putting together, taking apart, and comparing, with unknowns in all positions.

Appendix C

Vocabulary/Word Wall by Chapter

Chapter 1

Landforms

Observe

World

Chapter 2

Man-made

Natural

Chapter 3

Experiment

Natural process

Sprout

Chapter 4

Conclusion

Experiment

Hypothesis

Results

Scientific method

Scientist

Chapter 5

Gas

Liquid

Matter

Property

Solid

State

Chapter 6

Mixture

Solution

Chapter 7

Acceleration

Mass

Weight

Chapter 8

Balance

Gravity

Decelerate

Chapter 9

Energy

Force

Motion

Chapter 10

Inclined plane

Lever

Pulley

Screw

Simple machine

Wedge

Wheel and axle

Chapter 11

Attract

Magnet

Repel

Chapter 12

Pattern

Phases

Rotation

Chapter 13

Air pollution

Solar

Solar system

Chapter 14

Atmosphere

Cloud

Condensation

Evaporation

Water cycle

Weather

Chapter 15

Erosion

Weathering

Chapter 16

Core

Crust

Mantle

Chapter 17

Earthquake

Eruption

Lava

Magma

Plates

Shifting

Volcano

Chapter 18

Igneous rock

Metamorphic rock

Sediment

Sedimentary rock

Chapter 19

Decompose

Organism

Soil

Chapter 20

Biodegradable

Environment

Landfills

Polluted

Recycle

Reduce

Reuse

Chapter 21

Carnivores

Consumers

Food chain

Herbivores

Omnivores

Producers

Chapter 22

Ecosystem

Endangered species

Habitat

Chapter 23

Senses

Chapter 24

Amphibians

Class

Classify

Evolved

Fish

Gills

Invertebrate

Mammal

Reptile

Spine

Vertebrae

Vertebrate

Chapter 25

Life cycle

Nutrients

Reproduction

Appendix D

Activity Sheets and Posters

Contents

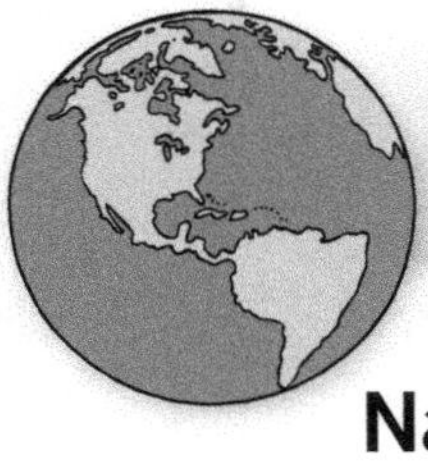

My World

Name ____

 ©2014 Kaye Hagler from *Inquire, Investigate, Integrate*. This page may be reproduced for classroom use only.

Match the Landform

Name ______________________________

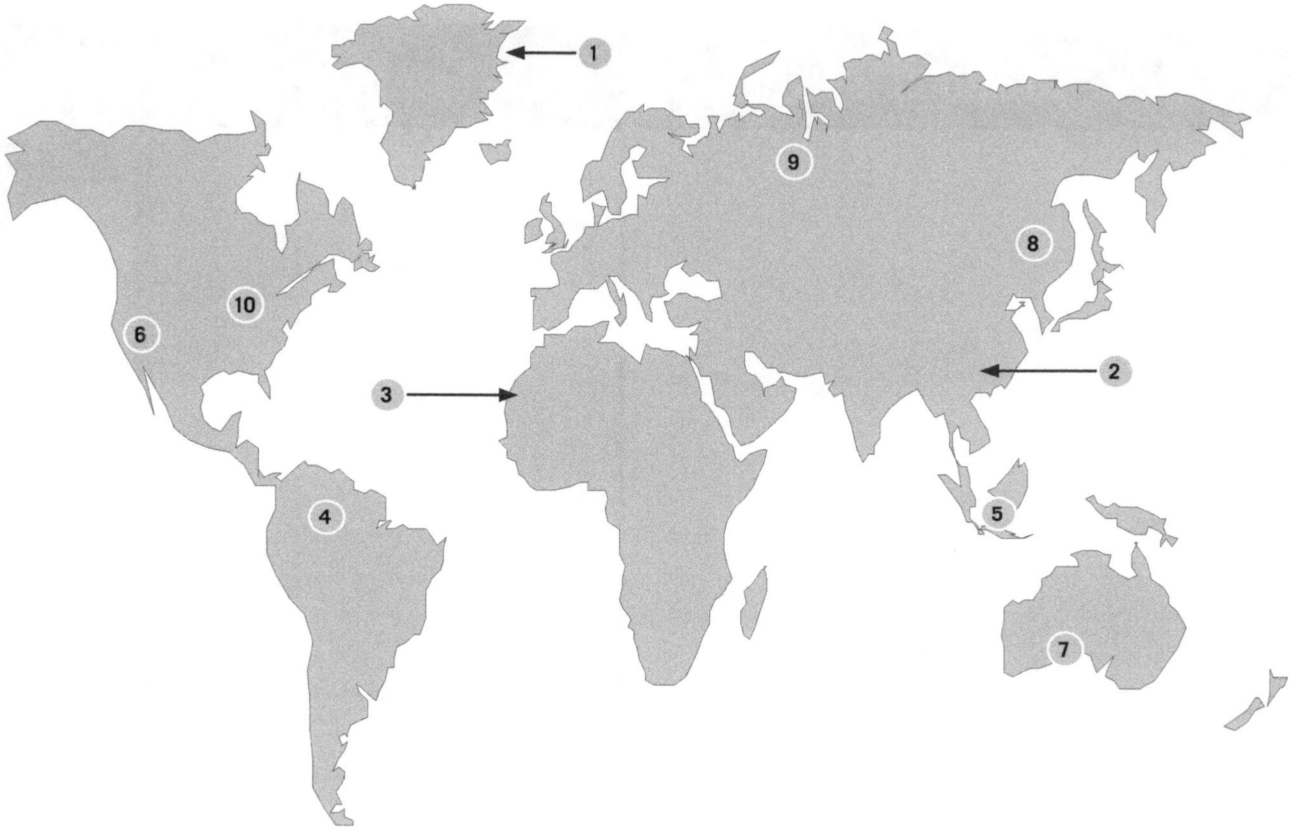

1 — glacier
2 — mountain
3 — desert
4 — river
5 — rain forest
6 — desert
7 — grassland
8 — river
9 — mountain
10 — plain

grassland plain desert mountain rain forest river glacier

©2014 Kaye Hagler from *Inquire, Investigate, Integrate*. This page may be reproduced for classroom use only.

Natural / Man-Made

Name ______________________________

Natural	Man-Made

©2014 Kaye Hagler from *Inquire, Investigate, Integrate*. This page may be reproduced for classroom use only.

Science Experiment: Natural vs. Man-Made Sponges

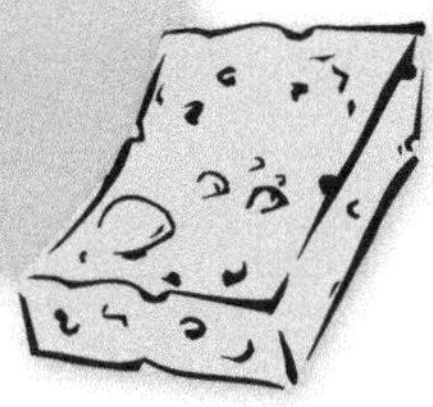

Name ______________________________

	Natural	Man-Made
Softness Test		
Smell Test		
Soaking Test		

©2014 Kaye Hagler from *Inquire, Investigate, Integrate*. This page may be reproduced for classroom use only.

Natural Process: Seeds Sprouting

Name ______________________________

Check the seeds each day. Describe or draw any changes in the seed.

Day 1	Started the test.
Day 2	
Day 3	
Day 4	
Day 5	
Day 6	
Day 7	

©2014 Kaye Hagler from *Inquire, Investigate, Integrate*. This page may be reproduced for classroom use only.

Scientific Method poster

Scientific Method

- Observe a problem
- Ask a Question
- Form a Hypothesis (possible answer)
- Conduct an Experiment
- Study the Results
- State a Conclusion

©2014 Kaye Hagler from *Inquire, Investigate, Integrate*. This page may be reproduced for classroom use only.

Scientific Method

Name ____________________

1. ____________________

2. ____________________

3. ____________________

4. ____________________

5. ____________________

6. ____________________

 ©2014 Kaye Hagler from *Inquire, Investigate, Integrate.* This page may be reproduced for classroom use only.

Cleaning Up Dirt and the Scientific Method

Name____

1. What's the Big problem?

2. How can I solve this problem?

3. The two items I chose for my experiment:

4. Circle the number to show the success of the experiment.

1. Very successful
2. OK
3. Could have been better
4. Did not work at all

5. What would I change to make the experiment better?

©2014 Kaye Hagler from *Inquire, Investigate, Integrate*. This page may be reproduced for classroom use only.

KWL Chart

Name ____

K	W	L

©2014 Kaye Hagler from *Inquire, Investigate, Integrate*. This page may be reproduced for classroom use only.

Three States of Matter poster

Gas

A gas is matter that takes the shape of
its container. Most gases cannot be seen.

Solid

A solid is matter that keeps its shape.
Its weight/mass can be measured.

Liquid

A liquid is matter that takes the shape of
its container. Its weight/mass can be measured.

©2014 Kaye Hagler from *Inquire, Investigate, Integrate*. This page may be reproduced for classroom use only.

Solids (b)

Name ______________________________

Select a marker, crayon, or colored pencil that matches your object. Draw a straight line in the space below using that color.

Circle the shape of your object.

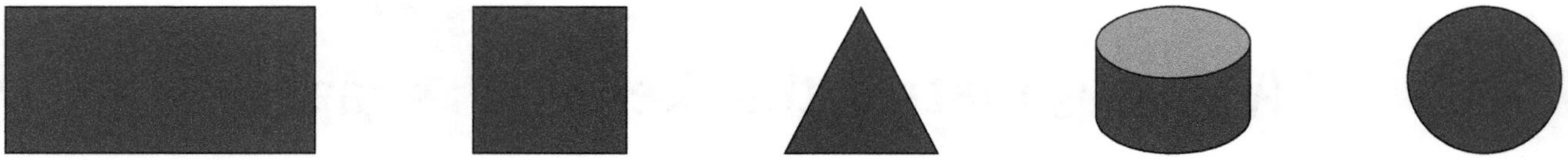

How tall is the object? ______________________________

How much does the object weigh? ______________________________

 ©2014 Kaye Hagler from *Inquire, Investigate, Integrate*. This page may be reproduced for classroom use only.

Solids (a)

Name____

Color	
Shape	
Height	
Weight	

©2014 Kaye Hagler from *Inquire, Investigate, Integrate*. This page may be reproduced for classroom use only.

Mixtures and Solutions

Name ____

In the first column, list the item you tested in each experiment.
Then, place a checkmark to show whether you created a mixture or a solution.

	Mixture	Solution
Experiment #1		
Experiment #2		
Experiment #3		

©2014 Kaye Hagler from *Inquire, Investigate, Integrate*. This page may be reproduced for classroom use only.

Measuring Mixtures and Solutions

Name____

$\frac{3}{3}$ →

$\frac{2}{3}$ →

$\frac{1}{3}$ →

©2014 Kaye Hagler from *Inquire, Investigate, Integrate*. This page may be reproduced for classroom use only.

Falling Objects

Name ______________________________

Record your results in the following manner:

- **List the two objects that were dropped in the first column.**
- **If the two objects fall at approximately the same time, place an = (equal sign) in the second column.**
- **If the two objects do not fall at approximately the same time, place an ≠ (unequal sign) in the third column.**

Objects Tested	=	≠

 ©2014 Kaye Hagler from *Inquire, Investigate, Integrate*. This page may be reproduced for classroom use only.

Sentence Cube Template

©2014 Kaye Hagler from *Inquire, Investigate, Integrate*. This page may be reproduced for classroom use only.

Impact! Measuring Craters

Name ______________________________

Dime, Nickel, Penny, Quarter

After dropping the object from the listed height, write (or draw) the coin that best represents the size of the crater created.

4 inches (10.2 cm)

8 inches (20.3)

12 inches (30.5 cm)

16 inches (40.6 cm)

Results

How did height affect the size of the crater?

Why did changing the height change the size of the crater?

 ©2014 Kaye Hagler from *Inquire, Investigate, Integrate*. This page may be reproduced for classroom use only.

Speed and Surface Challenge

Name ____

Surface	Time

Hypothesis: Which surface will be the fastest?

What was the result of the test?

How did different surfaces affect the speed?

©2014 Kaye Hagler from *Inquire, Investigate, Integrate*. This page may be reproduced for classroom use only.

Domino Math

Name ______________________________

______ + ______ = ______   ______ + ______ = ______   ______ + ______ = ______

______ + ______ = ______   ______ + ______ = ______   ______ + ______ = ______

______ + ______ = ______   ______ + ______ = ______   ______ + ______ = ______

 ©2014 Kaye Hagler from *Inquire, Investigate, Integrate*. This page may be reproduced for classroom use only.

Simple Machine poster

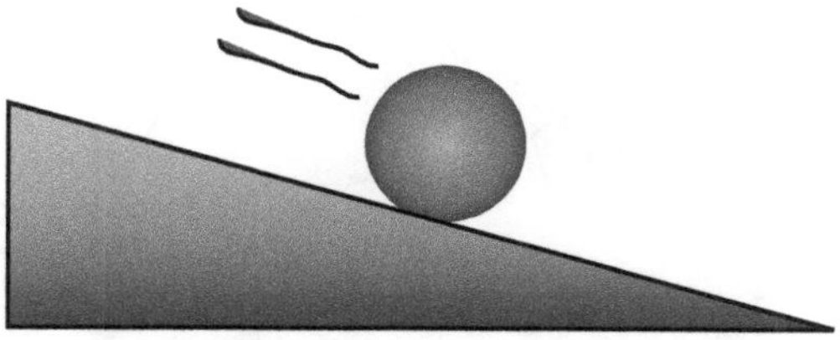

Inclined Plane

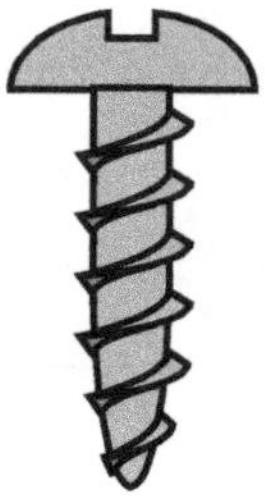

Screw

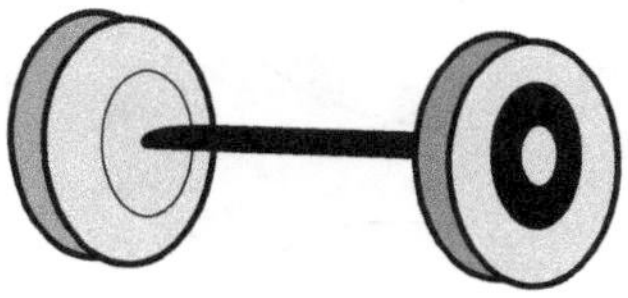

Wheel and Axle

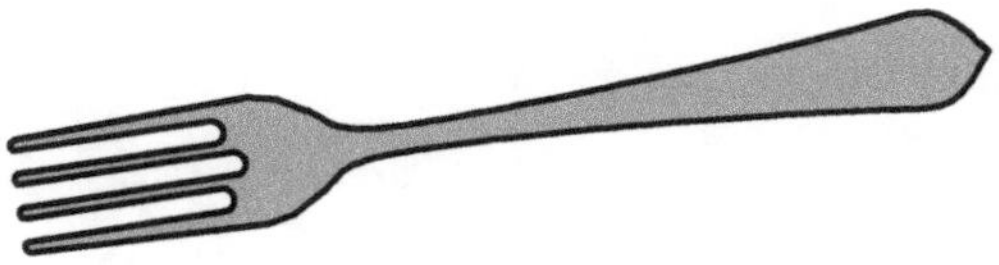

Wedge

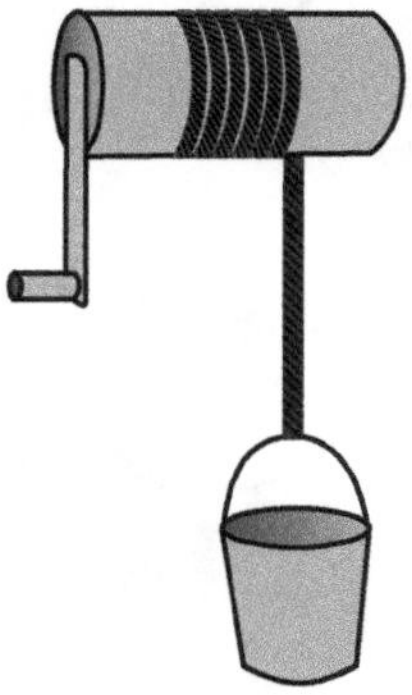

Pulley

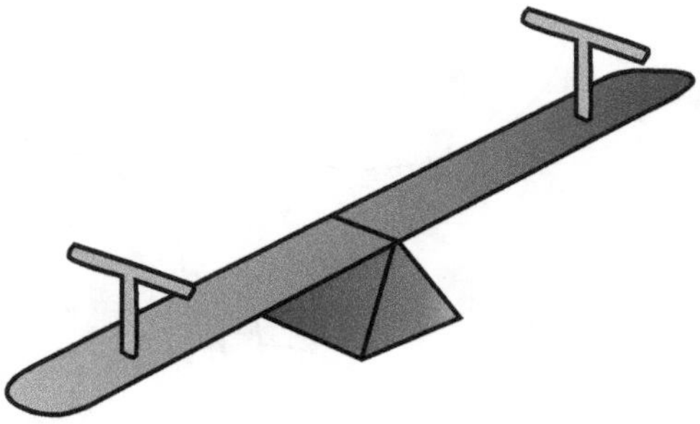

Lever

©2014 Kaye Hagler from *Inquire, Investigate, Integrate*. This page may be reproduced for classroom use only.

Cotton Ball Math

Name ____________________________________

8 – 3 = ______

2 + 7 = ______

4 + 3 = ______

1 + 6 = ______

7 + 3 = ______

 ©2014 Kaye Hagler from *Inquire, Investigate, Integrate*. This page may be reproduced for classroom use only.

Magnetic Attraction

Name ________________________________

Attracted	Not Attracted

©2014 Kaye Hagler from *Inquire, Investigate, Integrate*. This page may be reproduced for classroom use only.

Name ______________________________________

Let's Go Fishing for Math

 ©2014 Kaye Hagler from *Inquire, Investigate, Integrate*. This page may be reproduced for classroom use only.

The Man in the Moon

Name ______________________________

©2014 Kaye Hagler from *Inquire, Investigate, Integrate*. This page may be reproduced for classroom use only.

Fly to the Moon

Name ______________________________

Problem 4

15 + 5 = ____

Problem 3

7 + 3 = ____

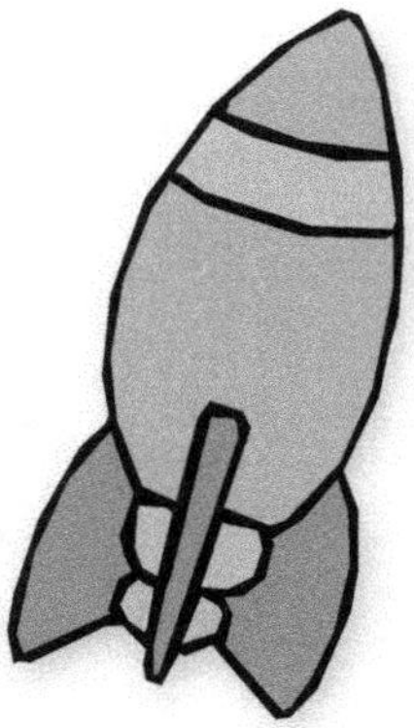

Problem 2

20 – 10 = ____

Problem 1

6 + 4 = ____

 ©2014 Kaye Hagler from *Inquire, Investigate, Integrate*. This page may be reproduced for classroom use only.

Power of the Sun

Name____

©2014 Kaye Hagler from *Inquire, Investigate, Integrate*. This page may be reproduced for classroom use only.

Melting Ice

Name ____

Time: ____

Description: ____

Time: ____

Description: ____

Time: ____

Description: ____

Time: ____

Description: ____

Conclusion: ____

____

____

 ©2014 Kaye Hagler from *Inquire, Investigate, Integrate*. This page may be reproduced for classroom use only.

Air Pollution Pie Chart

Name ____

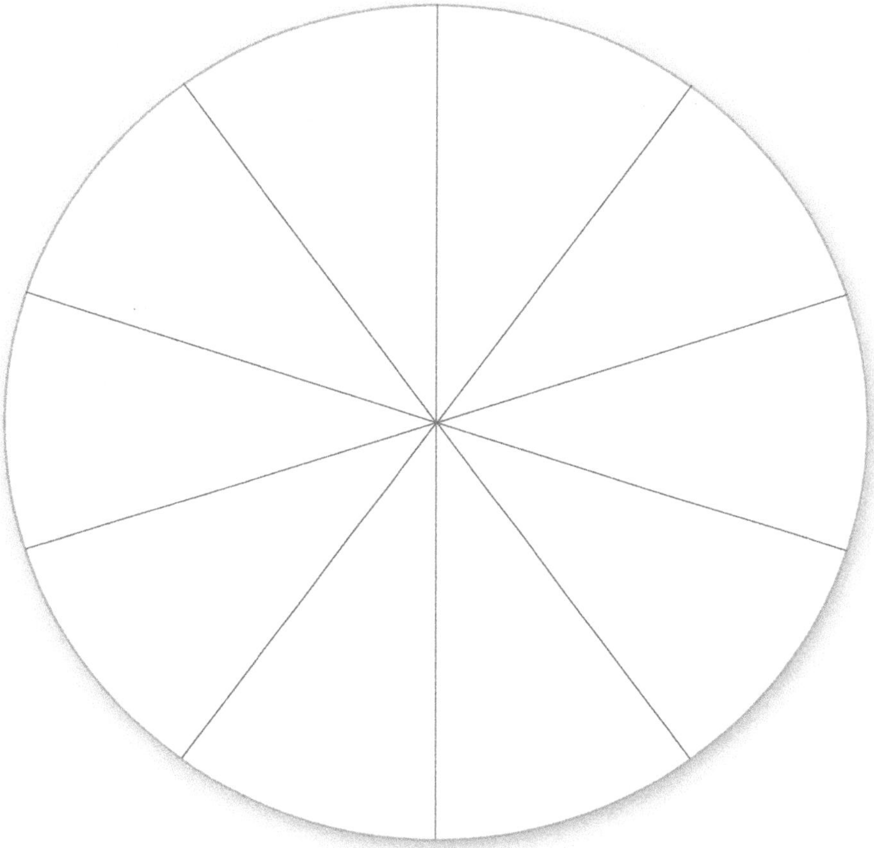

Color the Pie Chart

50%	Cars, trucks, and other transportation Color 5 of the slices blue.
30%	Factories Color 3 of the slices red.
20%	Homes and businesses Color 2 of the slices yellow.

Add the percentages: ______

©2014 Kaye Hagler from *Inquire, Investigate, Integrate*. This page may be reproduced for classroom use only.

Water Cycle

Name ____

 ©2014 Kaye Hagler from *Inquire, Investigate, Integrate*. This page may be reproduced for classroom use only.

Homophones

Name ____

Complete the word | Draw a picture of

R ____ ____ N falling **rain**

R ____ ____ N a horse and a rein

S ____ ____ a choppy **sea**

S ____ ____ something special your eyes can see

S ____ ____ a bright **sun**

S ____ ____ a parent's young boy

M ____ ____T **mist** (water droplets)

M ____ ____ ____ E D missed the bus

R ____ ____S the sun's **rays**

R ____ ____ ____ E D raised a flag

©2014 Kaye Hagler from *Inquire, Investigate, Integrate.* This page may be reproduced for classroom use only.

World of Rocks

Name____

Rock 1

____

____

____

Rock 2

____

____

____

Rock 3

____

____

____

 ©2014 Kaye Hagler from *Inquire, Investigate, Integrate*. This page may be reproduced for classroom use only.

Layers of the Earth

Name ______________________________

Label the layers of the Earth.

Core, Mantle, Crust

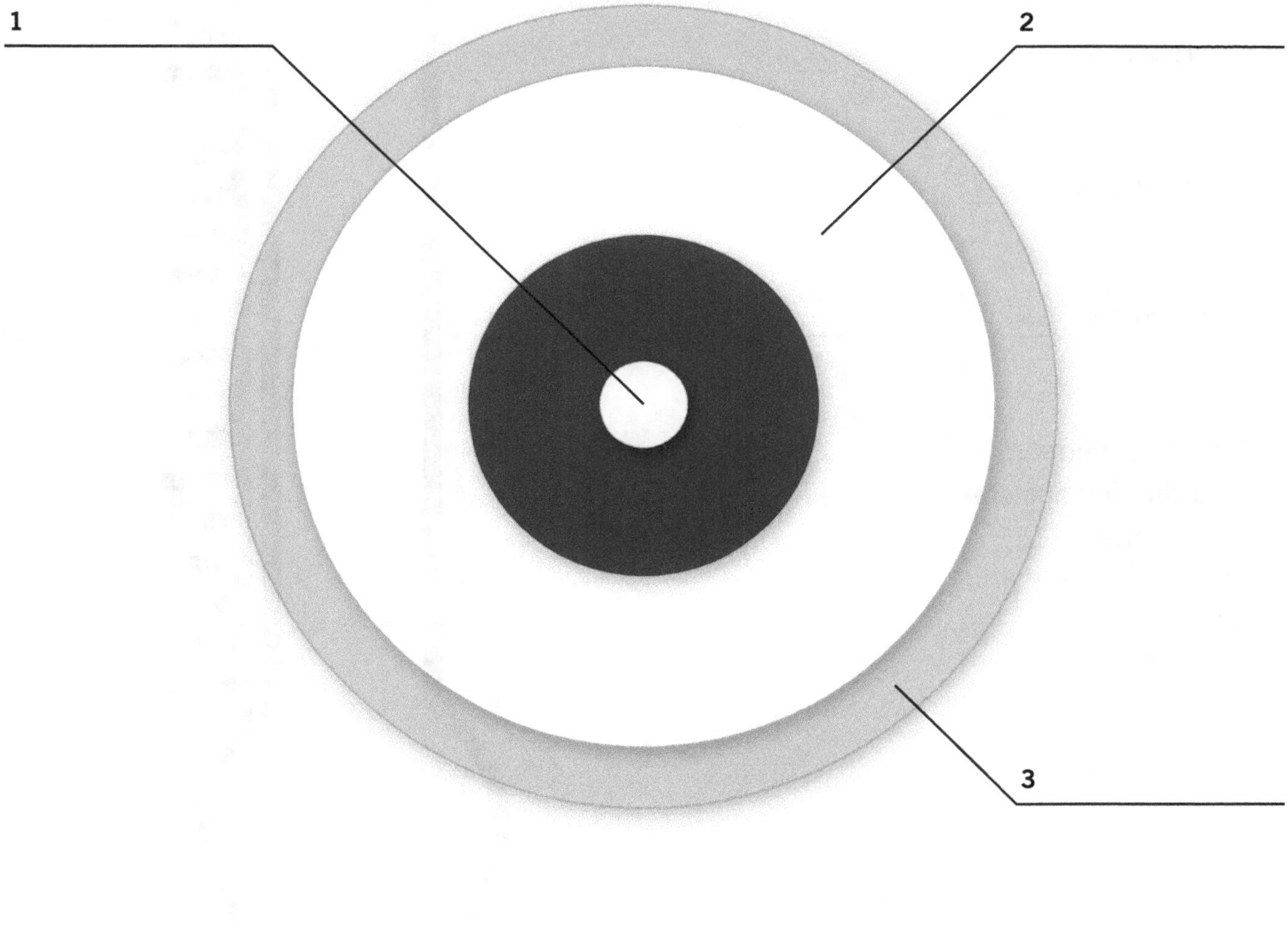

©2014 Kaye Hagler from *Inquire, Investigate, Integrate*. This page may be reproduced for classroom use only.

Thermometer Graph

Name ______________________________________

Record the results for each container.

Experiment 1: ______________________

Experiment 2: ______________________

Experiment 3: ______________________

Experiment 4: ______________________

Use these colors to color the thermometer:

Red—hottest
Orange
Yellow
Blue—coolest

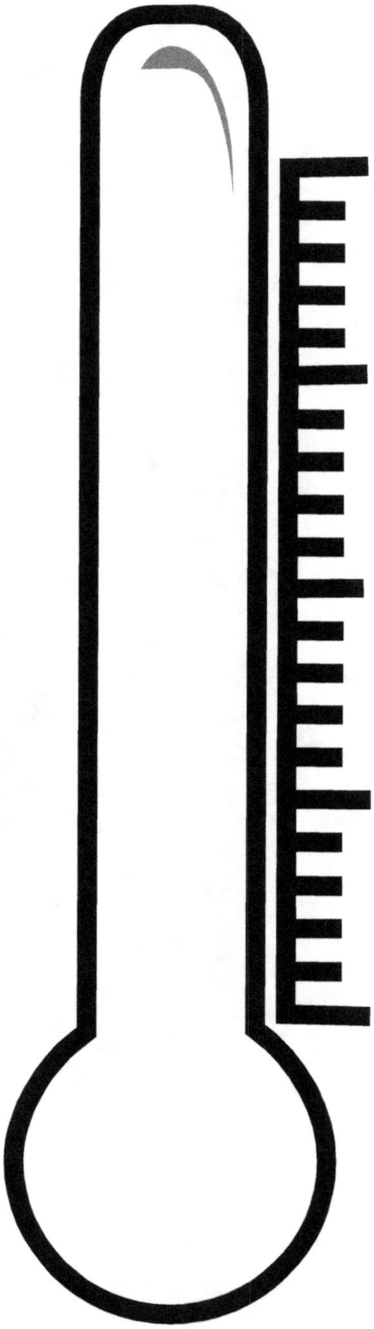

 ©2014 Kaye Hagler from *Inquire, Investigate, Integrate*. This page may be reproduced for classroom use only.

Soil Samples

Name ______________________________

Soil Sample Letter: ______	
Appearance (colors, objects visible)	Texture (clumps, gritty, smooth)
How well it holds water	Smell

©2014 Kaye Hagler from *Inquire, Investigate, Integrate*. This page may be reproduced for classroom use only.

Soil Mixtures and Plant Growth

Name ____

Sample 1	Sample 2

Results

Which sample held water for the longest period of time?

Why?

 ©2014 Kaye Hagler from *Inquire, Investigate, Integrate*. This page may be reproduced for classroom use only.

Food Chain

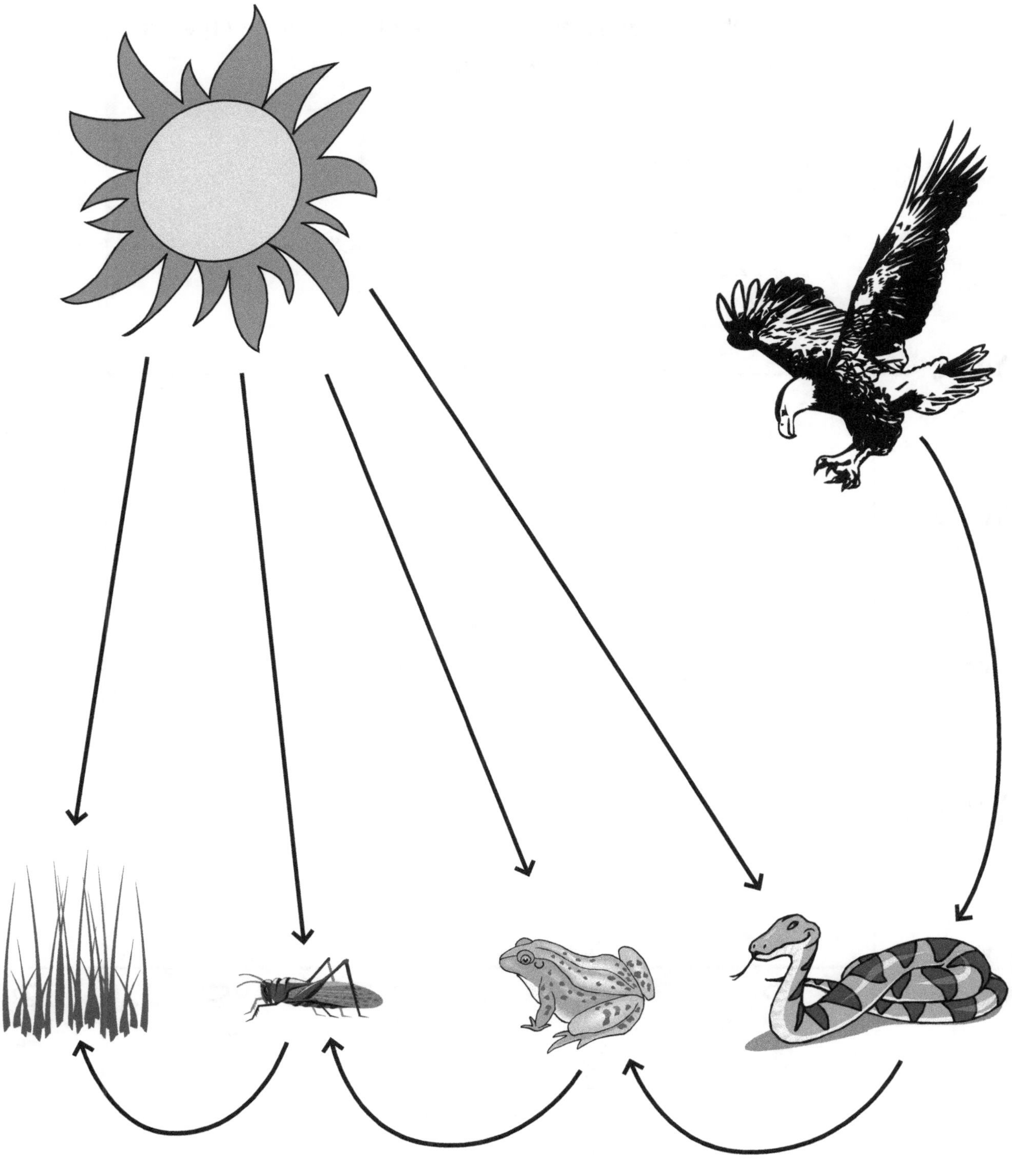

©2014 Kaye Hagler from *Inquire, Investigate, Integrate*. This page may be reproduced for classroom use only.

Life Span Bar Graph

Name ____

Using the data given on the average life span of an organism, represent the data on a bar graph.

Average Life Span
Camel: 40 Years
Worker Bee: 1 Year
Cat: 15 Years
Dog: 20 Years
Goat: 10 Years

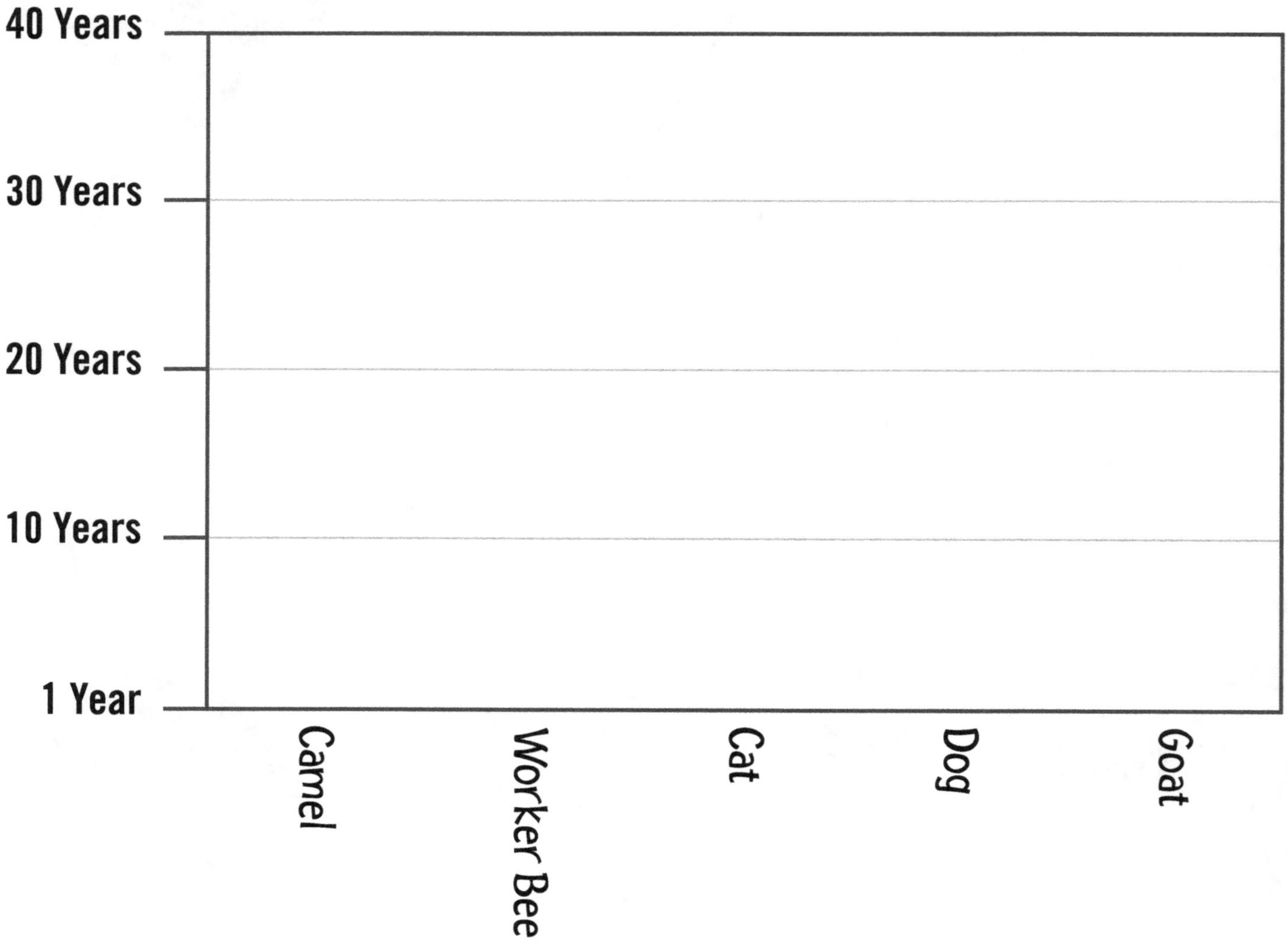

 ©2014 Kaye Hagler from *Inquire, Investigate, Integrate*. This page may be reproduced for classroom use only.

My Ecosystem

Name ______________________________

Beginning Date: ______________________________

Materials Used: ______________________________

Amount: ______________________________

1st Observation: ______________________ **Date:** ________

2nd Observation: ______________________ **Date:** ________

3rd Observation: ______________________ **Date:** ________

©2014 Kaye Hagler from *Inquire, Investigate, Integrate*. This page may be reproduced for classroom use only.

Taste Sample 1

Name ____________________

Sample Number: ____________________

Appearance

5 — 4 — 3 — 2 — 1

Most Pleasing … Least Pleasing

Smell

5 — 4 — 3 — 2 — 1

Most Pleasing … Least Pleasing

Taste

5 — 4 — 3 — 2 — 1

Most Pleasing … Least Pleasing

Results

Which sample was preferred because of appearance? ____________

Because of smell? ____________________

Because of taste? ____________________

©2014 Kaye Hagler from *Inquire, Investigate, Integrate*. This page may be reproduced for classroom use only.

Thunderstorm Chart

Name ______________________________

__5__ seconds 1 mile away

_____ seconds 2 miles away

_____ seconds 3 miles away

_____ seconds 4 miles away

_____ seconds 5 miles away

_____ seconds 6 miles away

_____ seconds 7 miles away

_____ seconds 8 miles away

_____ seconds 9 miles away

_____ seconds 10 miles away

_____ seconds 11 miles away

_____ seconds 12 miles away

_____ seconds 13 miles away

_____ seconds 14 miles away

©2014 Kaye Hagler from *Inquire, Investigate, Integrate*. This page may be reproduced for classroom use only.

Spine Chart

Name ______________________________

Neck:	7 vertebrae
Chest:	12 vertebrae
Lower Back:	5 vertebrae
Sacrum:	5 fused vertebrae
Tailbone:	3 fused vertebrae

Color the Neck vertebrae BLUE.
Color the Chest vertebrae GREEN.
Color the Lower Back vertebrae RED.
Color the Sacrum vertebrae YELLOW.
Color the Tailbone vertebrae BLACK.

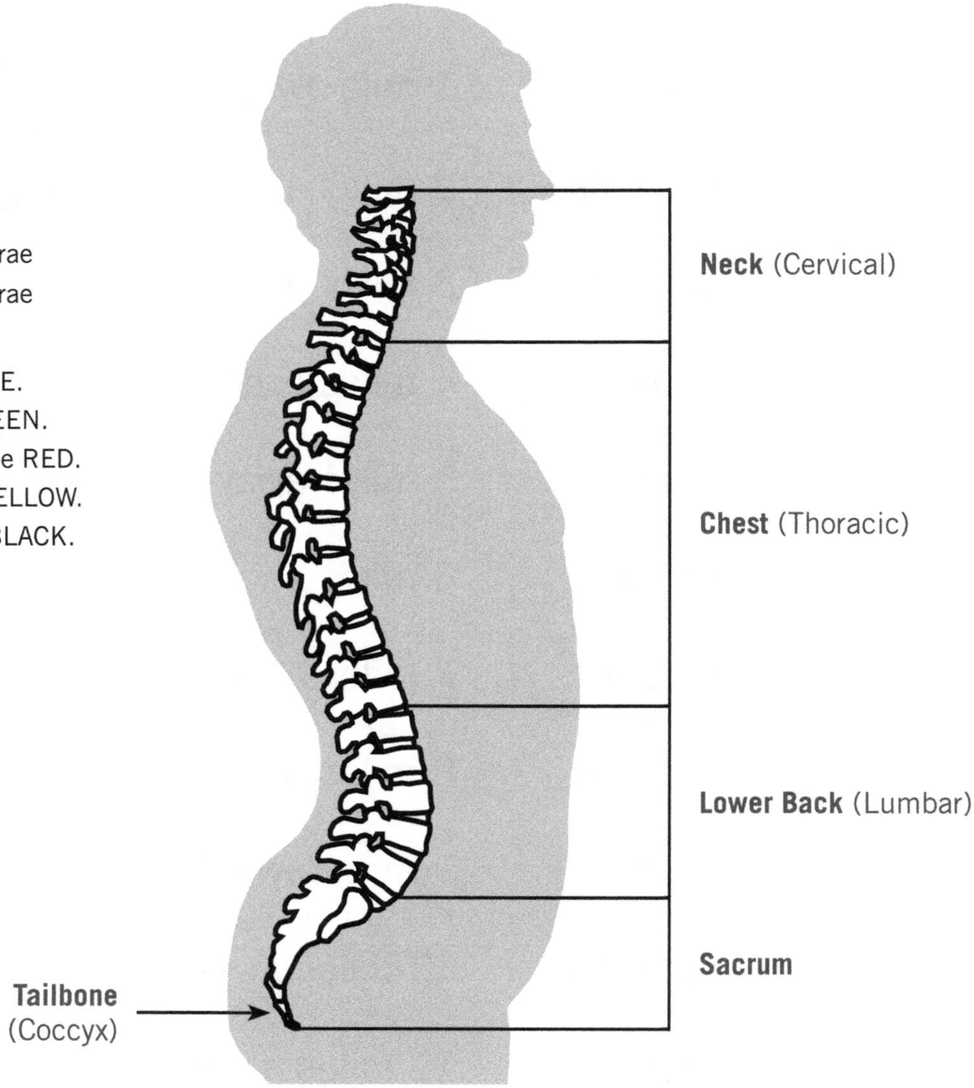

What is the total number of vertebrae? ________

How many more thoracic vertebrae are there than lumbar? ________

Cervical than sacrum? ________

©2014 Kaye Hagler from *Inquire, Investigate, Integrate*. This page may be reproduced for classroom use only.

Parts of the Flower

Name ______________________________

Write the correct label on the line to the left of the flower:

Roots

Stem

Leaves

Flower

What's My Job?

I make seeds so that more plants like me can grow. ____________________

I support the plant and keep it from falling over. ____________________

I soak up water and food, and then store them like a cupboard. ____________________

I work like a factory by making food. ____________________

I hold the plant in the ground. ____________________

I work like an elevator, carrying food up and down wherever it is needed. ____________________

I have tiny openings to let water and air come inside. ____________________

I attract bees, butterflies, and other insects. ____________________

©2014 Kaye Hagler from *Inquire, Investigate, Integrate*. This page may be reproduced for classroom use only.

Our Potato Patch

Name ______________________________

Type of Potato Selected:

____

Method of Sprouting:

____

Container Used:

____

Method of Planting Potato:

____

Medium Used to Grow Potato:

____

Additional Material Added to the Medium:

____

 ©2014 Kaye Hagler from *Inquire, Investigate, Integrate*. This page may be reproduced for classroom use only.